How Many Subjects?

Statistical Power Analysis in Research

Second Edition

Helena Chmura Kraemer
Stanford University

Christine Blasey
Palo Alto University

Los Angeles | London | New Delhi
Singapore | Washington DC | Boston

Los Angeles | London | New Delhi
Singapore | Washington DC | Boston

FOR INFORMATION:

SAGE Publications, Inc.
2455 Teller Road
Thousand Oaks, California 91320
E-mail: order@sagepub.com

SAGE Publications Ltd.
1 Oliver's Yard
55 City Road
London EC1Y 1SP
United Kingdom

SAGE Publications India Pvt. Ltd.
B 1/I 1 Mohan Cooperative Industrial Area
Mathura Road, New Delhi 110 044
India

SAGE Publications Asia-Pacific Pte. Ltd.
3 Church Street
#10-04 Samsung Hub
Singapore 049483

Copyright © 2016 by SAGE Publications, Inc.

Printed in the United States of America

Cataloging-in-publication data is available for this title from the Library of Congress.

ISBN 978-1-4833-1954-4

This book is printed on acid-free paper.

Acquisitions Editor: Helen Salmon
Assistant Editor: Katie Guarino
Editorial Assistant: Anna Villarruel
Production Editor: Laura Barrett
Copy Editor: Karin Rathert
Typesetter: C&M Digitals (P) Ltd.
Proofreader: Jennifer Grubba
Indexer: Jennifer Pairan
Cover Designer: Anupama Krishnan
Marketing Manager: Nicole Elliot

MIX
Paper from
responsible sources
FSC® C014174

15 16 17 18 19 10 9 8 7 6 5 4 3 2 1

How Many Subjects?

Second Edition

Table of Contents

List of Greek Symbols

Greek letters are here used to indicate population values that are sometimes estimated in the samples. It is useful to keep the distinction between an unknown population parameter and a sample of researcher-selected values.

Use	Greek Letter	Population Value	Sample Estimate
alpha	alpha	α	
regression parameter	beta	β	b
chi-square test statistic or distribution	chi-square	χ^2	
delta	delta lower case	δ	d
indicator of effect size/ design parameters	delta upper case	Δ	
error term	epsilon	ε	
lambda	lambda	λ	
mean	mu	μ	$\bar{x}$
indicator of necessary sample size	nu	ν	
standard normal cumulative distribution	phi upper case	Φ	
proportion	pi	$\pi, \pi'=1-\pi$	$p, q=1-p$
correlation coefficient	rho	ρ	r
standard deviation	sigma	σ	s
variance	sigma squared	σ^2	s^2

Preface to the Second Edition

In the preface to the first edition of this book (1987), we acknowledged the valuable contributions of Jacob Cohen[1], whose book on statistical power, even today, some 20 years after his death, remains arguably the best text on that issue. His influence on statistical methods in both psychology and medicine, particularly his efforts to emphasize the crucial role that statistical power plays on success in testing research hypotheses, remains strong. The first edition of this book was written on his suggestion, in an effort to simplify the application of statistical power.

Shortly before his death, I (HCK) met Jack face-to-face for the first time at a meeting of a subcommittee of the American Psychological Association that was jocularly called "The committee to ban the p-value." The committee did not actually recommend banning the p-value but emphasized how poorly statistical hypothesis testing was often done; how often p-values were overused, misused, and abused; and made recommendations to help repair the situation (summarized in the Wilkinson et al. paper[2]). In a side conversation with me, Jack lamented that his book on power and mine had probably done more harm than good in promoting better-designed studies. He pointed out how often those proposing research projects did power computations for one test but used another or did multiple power computations, apparently just to show they knew how to do such computations, that had no relevance to the design of the study proposed or simply misused the entire concept of power, often citing our books. Before our books were available, he suggested, researchers used common sense and knew, for example, that one could not draw valid inferences about heterogeneous populations with a sample size of 20. After our books became available, the same researchers would incorrectly use power calculations to propose a sample size of 20, citing our books for justification.

After my initial shock, I reluctantly came to agree with his assessment and long puzzled why this would be so. I finally came to the realization that we had put the primary, almost exclusive, emphasis on calculation of power, but calculation of power is meaningless and even misleading unless it is done within the proper context of statistical hypothesis testing and, even further, statistical hypothesis testing is meaningless and even misleading unless it is done within the proper context of the scientific method. Moreover, not only our books on power but, what is worse, many courses in statistics given to researchers in training put the primary, almost exclusive, emphasis on calculation. Students learn to "do" a two-sample t-test, a regression analysis, a 2 by 2 chi-square test, and so forth, with very little understanding of when each such test is appropriate or not.

This is like teaching a child to play baseball by teaching him to bat, throw, run, and field but never exposing that child to the rules of baseball or allowing him to interact with eight other players in an actual game. If, on the basis of such training, one were to ask that child to play in a game, he's not likely to do very well. Having all the basic skills without knowledge of the context or interactions necessary to the game will not serve him well. In the same way, teaching statistical test calculations in absence of knowledge of the "rules" of the scientific method or the "interaction" with sampling, design, and measurement issues does not equip researchers well to do valid and powerful scientific research. The problems are particularly salient in biobehavioral research, where research is done using living (human or animal) subjects rather than tissue samples or chemical reactions.

Consequently in this second edition, we begin with two new chapters, updating and replacing the original Chapters 1 (Introduction) and 2 (General Concepts) with one chapter setting statistical hypothesis-testing in the context of the scientific method as applied to biobehavioral research and another spelling out all the components of statistical hypothesis testing and where power considerations play a role. In these chapters, special attention is paid to the most common mistakes that we see in reviewing proposal or paper submissions or in publications.

The organization of the remaining chapters parallels those in the first edition, but often with new examples, with reference, where appropriate, to contextual issues, and with addition, where appropriate, to mistakes often made.

What we haven't changed are the tables—one set of tables that can be used for a variety of different common tests by modifying the relationship of the effect size, design parameters, and sample size to the row and column definitions. While there are many ways to implement power computations, including tables, nomograms, and computer packages, when times come for "what if" thinking in designing a study, being able to compare power with different designs all referring to the same set of tables still seems the easiest. However, even if users find they prefer using different tables, nomograms, or computer packages to do power computations (to be honest, both of the present authors use these tables for teaching but not usually in designing studies), the logic of the materials in each chapter will, we think, serve them well in using such alternative methods.

One reviewer of the first edition of this book suggested that readers borrow a library copy of the book, read through the book, then copy out the dozen pages of tables, in which case they would need not to buy the book. The reviewer was right. We hope that with the second edition many will note that the text is valuable whether or not one uses the tables.

In his foreword to the first edition, the late Victor H. Denenberg, then at the University of Connecticut, commented, "If this book only presented the reader with a straight-forward set of procedures for determining N (sample size) for any particular research design, it would have fulfilled its mission successfully. But the book does more. In the course of discussing different designs, the authors make note of important points that are of value to the empirical researcher. These include: the conditions under which a repeated measures design will be more or less efficient than a cross-sectional design; the considerations involved in deciding to match or stratify subjects; the selection of variables for a multiple regression analysis; the value of equal (or near equal) N in analysis of variance designs; how to insure, in a correlational study, that the study will be valid; and the N required to make a reasonably rigorous test of one hypothesis using the chi-square technique." In short, one of the advantages of our approach is what would correspond to "differential diagnosis" in medicine, the process here of sifting through various valid options available for testing a hypothesis and choosing the one most likely to succeed. Even greater stress will be placed on such "differential design diagnosis" in this edition.

We wish to thank the many researchers at Stanford University (particularly, but not exclusively, those in the Department of Psychiatry and Behavioral Sciences), at the University of Pittsburgh (Department of Psychiatry), and the researchers at other universities and in research organizations with whom we have worked over the years, who have made us aware of the importance of cost-effective research and the challenges inherent in trying to produce such research. We continue to acknowledge the influence of Jacob Cohen and of all those who read, commented on, and often criticized the limitations of the first edition. We would also especially acknowledge and appreciate the contribution of Sue Thiemann, who coauthored the first edition. Without her contributions to the first edition, clearly, this second edition would be impossible.

REFERENCES

1.   Cohen J. (1988). *Statistical power analysis for the behavioral sciences.* Hillsdale, NJ: Lawrence Erlbaum.
2.   Wilkinson, L. and the Task Force on Statistical Inference. (1999). Statistical methods in psychology journals: Guidelines and explanations. *American Psychologist.* 54, 594–604.

Acknowledgments

S AGE and the authors gratefully acknowledge feedback from the following reviewers:

- Glen C. Gamst, University of La Verne
- Bryan Rooney, Concordia University College of Alberta
- Richard E. Strauss, Texas Tech University
- Rebecca Warner, University of New Hampshire

About the Authors

Helena Chmura Kraemer received her bachelor's degree in Mathematics from Smith College (Summa cum Laude, 1958), did her first year of graduate study in Statistics as a Fulbright scholar at the University of Manchester, England, and then completed her doctoral studies in the Department of Statistics, Stanford University (1963). She joined the Department of Psychiatry and Behavioral Sciences at Stanford in 1964. Her primary interests concern the applications of biostatistics in the behavioral areas of medicine. In 1964, that seemed largely concentrated in Psychiatry, but in the years since, she has worked in Cardiology, Pediatrics, Radiology, Oncology, etc., as behavioral issues have become more prominent in all areas of medicine. She is a Fellow of the American Statistical Association, and of the American College of Neuropsychopharmacology. She was elected a member of the Institute of Medicine, Academy of Sciences, in 2003. She was also the recipient of the Harvard Prize in Psychiatric Biostatistics and Epidemiology in 2001, and Andrew C. Leon Distinguished Career Award, ISCTM, 2014, and a Honorary Doctor of Science, Wesleyan University, 2014.

She has published more than 300 papers in peer-reviewed journals, numerous chapters in books, and 6 books. At various times, she has served as associate editor or on the editorial boards of, for example, *Statistics in Medicine*, *Psychological Methods*, *Archives of General Psychiatry*, *Medical Decision Making*, and is a frequent reviewer for journals in Statistics, Psychiatry, and other fields of medicine.

Over the years before retirement in 2007, she mentored many young investigators both at Stanford, Pittsburgh, and other universities, providing training in research methods, as well as consultation on their proposals.

Her major current research interests concern the use of statistical methods in risk research, specifically the focus on moderators and mediators, the use of effect sizes to indicate clinical or practical significance to replace the overuse and abuse of statistical significance, and, in general, identifying and trying to rectify common problems in the application of statistical methods in medicine. She became Emerita in 2007, but continued to be active, serving on the NIMH council until 2008, and on the DSM-5 Task Force until 2012.

Christine Blasey is a Professor of Psychology at Palo Alto University and a Research Psychologist at Stanford University School of Medicine Department of Psychiatry and Behavioral Sciences. Christine received a Ph.D. in Psychology from the University of Southern California and an M.S. in Epidemiology from Stanford University. Christine provides statistical consultation in academic settings (e.g., Departments of Psychiatry, Cardiovascular Medicine, Education) and in the private sector for pharmaceutical companies testing new medicines and medical devices. Christine's consultation area of expertise is the interaction between pharmaceutical companies and the United States Food and Drug Administration (FDA). She has co-authored over fifty peer-reviewed journal articles and book chapters and serves as a statistical reviewer for several psychology and psychiatry journals. Christine teaches statistics, research methods, and psychometrics in the PGSP-Stanford University Consortium for Clinical Psychology. Her primary interest is mentoring future psychologists.

1

The "Rules of the Game"

The "game" of interest here is the use of the scientific method to establish scientific facts, at least as it might be applied in biobehavioral research. According to the Oxford English Dictionary, the scientific method is defined as "a method or procedure that has characterized natural science since the 17th century, consisting in systematic observation, measurement, and experiment, and the formulation, testing, and modification of hypotheses." The focus here is on the testing of hypotheses using the methods of statistical hypothesis testing that have been in use since early in the 20th century, but statistical hypothesis testing can only be successful within the framework of the scientific method in general. One view of the scientific method, as applied to biobehavioral research, is shown in Figure 1.0.

1.1 Exploratory Studies

Every study begins with exploration. Exploratory studies include review of the relevant literature, consideration of theories current in the relevant field, incorporation of clinical experiences and observations, secondary data analysis of data from earlier studies, and when one is close to the cutting edge of science and little is known about the relevant field, perhaps even research studies designed and executed specifically for exploration. Exploratory studies are efforts to find out what is going on in a particular area and are not designed to address specific a priori hypotheses. Usually there is no data analytic plan—the analyses done are inspired and guided by data. It is not unusual that one analyzes data in a variety of different ways, trying out different models and approaches. It is not unusual that one sees patterns that are completely unexpected that inspire ideas completely different from those that initiated the study.

What emerges from exploratory studies are not conclusions. The primary goal of such exploratory studies is to generate the theoretical rationale and the

Figure 1.0 The Process of the Scientific Method

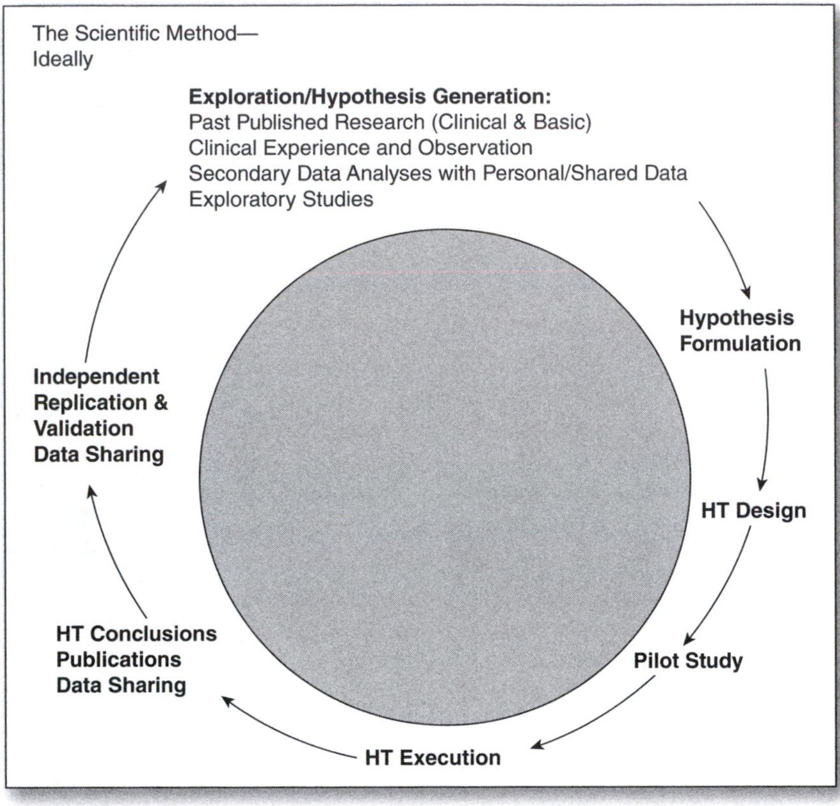

The Scientific Method—
Ideally

Exploration/Hypothesis Generation:
Past Published Research (Clinical & Basic)
Clinical Experience and Observation
Secondary Data Analyses with Personal/Shared Data
Exploratory Studies

**Hypothesis
Formulation**

**Independent
Replication &
Validation
Data Sharing**

HT Design

**HT Conclusions
Publications
Data Sharing**

Pilot Study

HT Execution

HT = Hypothesis Testing

empirical justification for proposing a certain hypothesis to be tested in a subsequent hypothesis-testing study designed for that purpose. From an exploratory study, there should be enough evidence to make it reasonable that the hypothesis proposed is true, and if true, of some importance. But there should not be enough evidence to assure its truth. This balance is often called *equipoise* (Freedman, 1987).

Equipoise is crucial, particularly in dealing with human subjects in research studies. Clinical equipoise is often presented as an ethical issue, because, regardless of the research question, participation in a research study places a burden on human subjects, can, in some cases, endanger their health and well-being, and wastes time and money. However, equipoise is also a scientific issue. It is very difficult for a researcher who already "knows" what the "right" answer to a research question should be to design, execute, analyze, and interpret the results without a bias generated by that "knowledge."

Beyond rationale and justification for a hypothesis, a vitally important goal of such exploratory studies is to provide the information needed to design a valid and powerful study to test that hypothesis. In the process of designing a study, a myriad of questions arise: what sampling frame to use, what inclusion/exclusion criteria to set, whether it would be preferable to use a representative sample or to stratify or match subjects, whether the study can be cross sectional or needs to be longitudinal, what the appropriate outcome measures are—an endless list. The correct answer to any such questions in one research study may be the wrong one in another. The clues to the correct answers to such questions for each specific hypothesis lie in the exploratory studies done in the development of the hypothesis to be tested in the study.

This may seem esoteric and overly complicated, and perhaps a simple analogy might help. Consider the long-running TV show *Law & Order*. Exploration is the "law" half of the show: the gathering of evidence and information by the detectives, information that is necessary for the district attorney to bring charges and to initiate a trial. The trial by judge or jury (the "order" half) corresponds to hypothesis testing. Where or how the detectives look for such information is not set in stone: How and where information is gathered may vary widely from one case to another. However, the more information is gathered and the more dependable it is, the stronger the evidence to organize and support the trial. A strong body of evidence is needed to decide that it is worth going to trial, that is, deciding that a conviction might be obtained. Finally, if the decision is to go to trial, the better the chance of a successful result (conviction). The same is true of exploratory studies.

However convincing evidence is to the detectives or, for that matter, to the district attorney, it is *not* a guilty verdict. When charges are brought and the trial begins, there continues a presumption of innocence until the charges are proven beyond reasonable doubt in the judicial process—the law half of the TV show. In the same way, there are no strict guidelines governing how exploratory studies might be done. Once a researcher has completed a study and developed a hypothesis, he or she may decide to formally test that hypothesis. That hypothesis is assumed false until proven "beyond reasonable doubt" by statistical hypothesis testing. Even the best and most carefully executed exploratory studies often lead to hypotheses that are not true.

That raises the question as to whether the results of exploratory studies are publishable or not. Clearly reviews of the research literature on a particular issue are often published. When these are subjective reviews, they can be misleading: the choice of publications and the assessment and compilation of the evidence in such publications is affected by whatever biases the reviewers hold. In recent years, meta-analysis (Cooper & Hedges, 1994; Cumming, 2012; Jones,1995) has been proposed to deal with such problems. The meta-analysis is required to gather and report *all* research studies done on an issue, thus removing possible bias in choice of publications included. Computerized searches of the extant research literature have greatly facilitated this process.

Then the meta-analyst is required to separate the studies that are valid from those that are not and to focus only on the valid studies for analysis and conclusions. This is often difficult, since setting aside a study done by a colleague (who may later review papers and proposals of the meta-analyst!) as invalid presents, let us say, a social challenge. What has been proposed to avoid this problem is that the meta-analyst state a priori the criteria for a valid study and then give each study a score depending on how well that study satisfies the criteria. This way a completely invalid study might receive a score of zero and not influence the meta-analysis at all (the same as if it were set aside). The more valid studies would have greater weight in influencing the conclusions of the meta-analysis than those less valid. In the meantime, the scores for individual studies are not necessarily published, protecting the anonymity of those who publish invalid studies and the careers of those who do meta-analysis including such studies.

In any case, a well-done meta-analysis might be invaluable to researchers other than the researcher doing this as part of an exploratory study, and thus is highly publishable. Moreover, a well-done meta-analysis might well protect equipoise. The results of such a study might result in the conclusion that the hypothesis is not only true and important but already proven to be true and important in previous studies. Conversely, the hypothesis may or may not be true but already shown to be of trivial clinical or practical importance. In both such situations, the results of a well-done meta-analysis would disturb equipoise and encourage researchers to move on to other research questions. Alternatively, the result of meta-analysis might be an indication that there is still some chance that the hypothesis is true and of clinical or practical importance, but the accumulation of studies to date has not definitively established it as scientific fact. In this case, another study that might settle the issue, designed to avoid any pitfalls detected in earlier studies, would be of great value. Thus, well-done meta-analyses should be highly publishable.

Consider also an exploratory study at the cutting edge of science, where few previous studies exist. For example, is there a gene or a combination of genes or a brain area or combination of brain areas that predisposes individuals to cancer, depression, heart disease, autism, and so forth? No one really knows, and while there is a lot of discussion and there are many publications on such issues, no one has yet documented exactly what gene or combination or what brain area or combination identifies those at risk of such disorders. Researchers might well examine thousands of genes or voxels of brain scans to explore such possibilities, and they have. Currently such studies are often inappropriately presented as hypothesis testing (i.e., with thousands of hypotheses), but there are downsides to doing so, not the least of which are the often irreproducible findings. If clearly presented as exploratory, however, so that other researchers might combine relevant results with other sources of information to focus on some single combination of genes or single combination of brain areas associated with one disorder in order to design a valid and powerful study to test that specific hypothesis, such studies would prove valuable to fostering more rapid progress in the field.

Thus there are exceptions, but generally the results of exploratory studies guide the hypotheses and study designs only locally and are not publishable. The key issue in deciding what should be publishable is the value of what is published to other researchers in the field.

1.2 Hypothesis Formulation

Every proposal starts with a *hypothesis*, a theory based on the rationale and justification found in the exploratory studies. That theory would, in one way or another, advance science—why bother to put the time and effort into the proposal if that were not true? The exact formulation of the hypothesis is vitally important, since that is what subsequently dictates the design.

For example, if the hypothesis posits that Treatment A produces better outcomes than Treatment B in the population of those with the disorder, symbolically A > B, that is one hypothesis—a so-called *one-tailed hypothesis*. The justification for such a hypothesis is that there is no possibility that A produces outcomes inferior to B in the theory or literature and that, if a study were to produce such a result, it would be summarily dismissed as a failed study. There are situations in which one-tailed hypotheses are appropriate. For example, if A were an active treatment with preliminary evidence of effectiveness in the population of interest, and B an inert placebo, the result that an inert placebo would produce better outcomes than such an active treatment would be untenable, and a one-tailed hypothesis would be appropriate. More usually, the indication is that A > B, but there remains some possibility that A < B. In that case the hypothesis would be two-tailed (hypothesis A ≠ B): A and B produce different outcomes in this population.

There are researchers and statisticians who would never accept a one-tailed hypothesis. This is because a one-tailed hypothesis may be initially proposed, but when the result comes out "in the wrong direction," there is a switch to a two-tailed hypothesis or sometimes even a one-tailed hypothesis in the opposite direction "post hoc." This is like the prosecuting attorney, after the jury has returned a not guilty verdict on the charges, protesting that, while those particular charges might not be proven, the defendant is clearly guilty of other charges and should be held accountable. That doesn't work in a trial by jury and it doesn't work in statistical hypothesis testing.

The hypothesis is one positing that in a mixed-gender population with the disorder, A ≠ B, is different from the hypothesis that A ≠ B both in men and in women. To take an unusual example, if A > B for women and A ≤ B for men in a population with about half men and half women, the overall outcome might well be A = B in the mixed-gender population, since the opposite effects for men and women might cancel out.

The simple fact is that the tests for A > B are different from those for A ≠ B and the tests for either of these situations in the general population are different from those specifying a certain hypothesis separately among men and women. In short, the exact specification of what you want to prove makes all the difference in the research design and all the difference in determining how many subjects are needed to adequately address that question.

1.3 The Null Hypothesis

Whatever the hypothesis proposed, the *null hypothesis* is the denial of that hypothesis. Thus if the hypothesis declares that A > B (one-tailed test), then the null hypothesis is A < B. If the hypothesis declares that A ≠ B, the null hypothesis is A = B. If the hypothesis is that A > B for both men and women, then the null hypothesis is that A < B for either men or women (or for both). The null hypothesis corresponds to the "innocence" in the *Law & Order* lexicon.

1.4 Design

Once one has formulated a hypothesis, with the theoretical rationale and empirical justification culled from exploratory studies, and convinced oneself that the hypothesis, if true, would be of clinical or practical importance, one then designs a study to test that hypothesis.

There are a myriad of questions that arise in designing such a study. Are you to sample one population, or do you need to have a control or comparison group? If so, what is an appropriate control group? What should be the inclusion/exclusion criteria for sampling into the study? Should the sample be a representative one from the population of interest, or should one stratify or match subjects? If there is a longitudinal follow-up, how long should that be? During that follow-up, how many times should the participants be seen and on what schedule? What information must be obtained from each participant to address the research question and when, and what instruments should be used to get that information? Which statistical tests should be used? And only when all such questions are answered, **how many subjects are needed to assure that, if the hypothesis is both true and of clinical or practical importance,**

the study will support that hypothesis? That last question is the topic of this book, but it can only be answered after the hypothesis is clearly articulated, the research design to address that hypothesis is known to be valid, and the specific statistical test that is to be used is known. Often in the design phase, there are several different designs, all specific to the hypothesis of interest and all valid, and several different tests to be considered. Then the methods of this book might be used to evaluate which of these valid designs would be more efficient, take least time, cost least money, minimize the burden and risk to participants, and so forth, to guide the final choice of design.

In *Law & Order*, this design phase corresponds to the DA's planning for a trial, the decisions of which evidence will be presented in which order, which witnesses will be called and in which order, and what the attorneys will question the witnesses about. Mistakes made at this stage may completely undermine the trial. Certain evidence, certain witnesses, and certain questions will be found inadmissible (validity), and poor presentation may not convince the judge or jury that the defendant's guilt is established beyond reasonable doubt (power).

1.5 The Statistical Test

A *statistical* test is a rule proposed a priori (before the data to which the test is to be applied are accessed) stipulating what has to be observed in the data to warrant rejection of the null hypothesis, which is often referred to as a "statistically significant" result (like a guilty verdict in the *Law & Order* lexicon).

What is required for a *valid* statistical test is a prespecified significance level—to define "reasonable level of doubt." The significance level is a cap on the probability of rejecting the null hypothesis when that null hypothesis is true. Thus, for a one-tailed test (hypothesis A > B), it is the maximal probability of rejecting that hypothesis in any situation when A≤B. For a two-tailed test (hypothesis A ≠ B), it is the probability of rejecting that hypothesis when A = B.

Generally the significance level is set at 5%. This is a matter of convention, an agreement that prevents proliferation of false positive findings misleading science. There are situations in which the significance level is set more stringently at 1%, and few would quibble with setting the significance level more stringently than convention requires.

Technically the significance level can be set at any value, provided only that it is set a priori. Thus, if in the proposal before the data used to test the theory are accessed, it is stated that the significance level to be used is 7%, from a statistical point of view, that is perfectly acceptable. Whether that is acceptable to colleagues in the field may be another matter. However, what often happens and is not acceptable is that the level is set at 5% a priori, but when the result of analyzing the data does not achieve that level but would achieve significance at the 7% level, a researcher nimbly proposes post hoc to change the significance level to 7%. That is unacceptable. Often such results are reported as "approaching significance" or "borderline significant"—all of which are nonsense phrases trying to conceal the fact that the researcher has *not* proven his or her theory, according to the standards of proof he or she accepted a priori. No, you can't change the rules of the game once you see what the outcome of the game is!

In a randomized clinical trial in which N subjects are to be sampled from a specified population and randomly assigned NP to A and NP' (P' = 1 − P) to B in order to compare outcomes in A and B, one might propose to compute the mean response to A (M_A) and to B (M_B) and the pooled within-group standard deviation s_p, and to reject the null hypothesis that A < B if the t-statistic t = $(NPP')^{1/2}(M_A - M_B)/s_p$ is greater than the 95th percentile of the central-t distribution with (N − 2) degrees of freedom. Or one might compute the absolute value of t and reject the null hypothesis that A = B if that is greater than the 97.5th percentile of the central-t distribution with (N − 2) degrees of freedom. Those are two different statistical tests.

These particular tests are taught in every elementary statistics course as the two-sample t-test (one-tailed or two-tailed). Elementary statistics textbooks usually have a table of the percentiles of the central-t distribution to facilitate the use of the test. Every statistical package has a program for executing this test, including calculation of the *p*-value. The *p*-value is a statistic computed from the data of the study that indicate the upper limit of the probability of obtaining the computed test statistic when the null hypothesis is true. Thus, if the *p*-value is below the a priori significance level α, the result is what is usually meant by "statistically significant at the α-level." Note that the significance level is a standard set a priori, while the *p*-value is a statistic computed from the data used to test the hypothesis, which is to be compared with the α-level to determine whether or not the hypothesis is supported by the data.

What was said above might seem cumbersome and unfamiliar, but that is only because what is usually said is something more like, "We will use a (one-tailed or two-tailed) t-test with a 5% level of significance to compare the A and B treatments," and such a phrase conveys all the above.

As is true of any statistical test, the t-test is based on certain assumptions about the population(s), in this case that the outcomes in both the A and B treatment groups have normal distributions with equal variances. Under these assumptions, a statistician writing under the pseudonym "Student" demonstrated more than a century ago that the t-test is valid at the α-level. Thus if the *p*-value computed for the t-test statistic is less than α, we have a statistically significant result and support for the theory. The validity of the test depends on how well the population sampled satisfies these assumptions. In the case of the t-test, if the outcomes measured are two-, three-, four-, . . . point scales or if the distribution of outcomes in one or the other treatment group is skewed or long tailed, that is, not normal distributions, proposing a two-sample t-test may lead to invalid results. If the outcome measure distribution is at least approximately normal in both groups but the variances are very different, again proposing a two-sample t-test may lead to invalid results. It is the responsibility of the researchers to check those assumptions before proposing to use any test and the responsibility of a statistical consultant to bring those assumptions to the attention of the researchers.

So what happens if the t-test assumptions are not likely to hold? Then, the researchers might prefer to propose to use a one-tailed or two-tailed Mann-Whitney test, which does not require normal distributions or equal variances but does require ordinal measures. If the outcomes are binary (success/fail), one might prefer to use a one- or two-tailed binomial test. Both of these tests also are commonly available in textbooks and statistical packages. In fact, for any hypothesis to be tested, there are numerous statistical tests, those in standard textbooks and those less commonly seen, that various researchers or statisticians might propose. Which should the researchers choose?

First and foremost is establishing the validity of the test. For a 5% level test, if there are situations consistent with the null hypothesis that will lead to statistically significant results with greater than a 5% probability, that test must be rejected from consideration as invalid. That cuts down the number of tests available for any hypothesis considerably but will still leave options. That's where power and the issues discussed in this book *How Many Subjects?* come into the picture, but to understand the issue of power, it is first necessary to understand effect sizes.

1.6 Effect Sizes: Critical, True, and Estimated

An *effect size* is a population parameter that indicates how strong the hypothesis is. For example, in comparing Treatments A and B, one might propose as an effect-size:

Probability (A > B) + .5 Probability (A = B), that is, the probability that if one randomly sampled one patient given A and one given B, that the one given A has an outcome preferable to the one given B (ties broken by a toss of a fair coin) (Kraemer & Kupfer, 2006). This effect size is often labeled *AUC* (because of its relationship to the *area under the receiver operating curve*). Then for the one-tailed hypothesis (A > B), the null hypothesis is AUC ≤ .5, and for the two-tailed hypothesis (A ≠ B), the null hypothesis is AUC = .5. AUC is an effect size closely associated with the Mann-Whitney test to compare A and B but can be used in any situation in which pairwise comparisons can be made and one outcome selected as preferable.

In the special case that outcomes in both A and B have normal distributions (with or without equal variances), one might propose another effect size:

Cohen's $\delta = (\mu_A - \mu_B)/\sigma_{AV}$, where μ_A is the population treatment mean for A, μ_B, the population treatment mean for B, and σ^2_{AV} is the average variance in the two treatment groups. (Note the use of Greek letters here to serve as a reminder that these are population means that can be estimated in a representative sample from that population but are never precisely known.) With two normal distributions, $AUC = \Phi(\delta/\sqrt{2})$, where $\Phi()$ is the cumulative normal distribution. Cohen's δ is the effect size associated with the two-sample t-test. In Table 1.6 below are shown what values of Cohen's δ (when the normality assumptions apply only) correspond to different values of AUC.

It is a matter of convenience and custom that the effect size used is zero or less when the null hypothesis is true. For Cohen's δ (when normality assumptions apply), the usual one- and two-tailed null hypotheses are in fact $\delta < 0$ and $\delta = 0$. However, expressed in terms of AUC, the null hypotheses would be $AUC < .5$ and $AUC = .5$, the cut-point non-zero. This problem is easily remedied by rescaling AUC to another effect size, SRD (success rate difference), equal to Probability

Table 1.6　Effect Size Equivalents: Cohen's Delta and Corresponding Areas Under the Curve (AUC)

Δ	AUC	SRD	NNT
Negative Infinity	0	−1	−1
−3	0.016947	−0.96611	−1.03508
−2.5	0.03855	−0.9229	−1.08354
−2	0.07865	−0.8427	−1.18666
−1.5	0.144422	−0.71116	−1.40616
−1	0.23975	−0.5205	−1.92123
−0.5	0.361837	−0.27633	−3.61891
0	0.5	0	Infinity
0.5	0.638163	0.276326	3.618909
1	0.76025	0.5205	1.92123
1.5	0.855578	0.711156	1.406162
2	0.92135	0.842701	1.186661
2.5	0.96145	0.9229	1.083541
Positive Infinity	1	1	1

(A > B) – Probability(A < B). The values of SRD that correspond to values of AUC (always) are also shown in Table 1.6. However, Cohen's δ, AUC, and SRD are not easily understood by clinicians or patients. Thus let us add one more possible effect size here.

Suppose you sampled NNT (number needed to treat) patients from each of the A and B populations and classified each patient as a success if she or he had an outcome preferable to a randomly selected patient in the other treatment (breaking any ties with a toss of a fair coin). How large must NNT be to have one more success among the A patients than among the B patients? A negative NNT indicates how large –NNT must be to have one more success among the B patients than among the A patients. NNT equals 1/SRD. (See Table 1.6 for how NNT relates to AUC and SRD always, and to Cohen's δ when comparing normal distributions.) Since NNT refers to patient counts rather than probability points, this effect size is often more interpretable for clinical applications. NNT is, however, extremely awkward in calculations because of its peculiar wraparound scale (See Table 1.6). As A gets better and better than B, NNT *decreases* from infinity to 1. As B gets better and better than A, NNT *increases* from negative infinity to –1, but having a negative "number" of patients is awkward. The notion that plus and minus infinity mean the same thing—that A is equivalent to B—is, to say the least, mathematically uncomfortable. However, one can always report the absolute value of NNT specifying whether A > B or B > A, and for computations one can convert NNT to SRD or to δ for normal distributions.

In recent years, there has been a great deal more emphasis on effect sizes (Acion, Peterson, Temple, & Arndt, 2006; Cumming, 2012; Ellis, 2010; Grissom & Kim, 2012; Kraemer & Kupfer, 2006; McGough and Faraone, 2009). The point here is that to any situation (here the comparison of Treatments A and B) there are a variety of possible effect sizes that can be used in any situation. Some, like Cohen's δ, only apply in certain situations. The trick is to pick one that can be interpreted in terms of clinical or practical importance and preferably one that eases power calculations.

All the above refers to the *population* effect size that is never known exactly. When the study is done, one can estimate population effect size along with some indication of the precision of estimation: a confidence interval or a standard error. There should always be a clear distinction between the *population* effect size and the estimated effect size. However, for purposes of design, we need yet another effect size, the *critical* effect size.

The critical effect size is the minimum value of the population effect size that would be clinically or practically significant. Take it as gospel that, as long as there is theoretical rationale and empirical justification from exploratory studies supporting a hypothesis to be formally tested, the population effect size is never absolutely zero, not out to the fifth or tenth or hundredth decimal place. However, the population effect size may be close enough to zero not to matter. For example, if a clinician would have to deliver a treatment to 2,500 patients to have one patient do better than if all 2500 were given an inactive placebo (NNT = 2500), will a clinician (or patient) be motivated to prefer that treatment? The answer may *be* yes if the treatment were the Salk vaccine against polio, where in fact the NNT is about 2500. However, what if the condition being treated were cancer and the treatment involved radiation and chemotherapy, with all the costs and risks they involve? Chances are, NNT = 2500 would be completely unacceptable to most clinicians and to most patients. What if then NNT = 4? If the control treatment were an inert placebo, in which case those treated with placebo might die—then even NNT = 4 might be unacceptable. One might then want NNT no greater than 1.5. If, however, the control treatment were an active treatment, the most effective known to date, then NNT = 4 might mean an amazing improvement over an already effective treatment, and so perhaps would be NNT = 9.

In short, the critical effect size in any particular situation depends on the nature of the population, the nature of the treatments being compared, the consequences of ineffective treatments, the costs and risks of such treatments, and so forth. It will change from one situation to another, and the sample size depends crucially on what the critical effect size is.

The critical effect size in any particular situation is determined by the exploratory analyses. In similar situations in the past, what magnitudes of effect sizes resulted in a shrug of the clinicians' shoulders, and what magnitudes resulted in the adoption of new treatments? It is a judgment call, but one informed by past experience.

Cohen, in his landmark book on statistical power (Cohen, 1988), suggested what magnitudes of various effect sizes might be considered "small," "medium," and "large." Thus, for example in comparing A versus B above, he suggested that δ = .2, .5, .8 might be the standards (SRD = .1, .3, .4, NNT = 9, 4, 2). In testing correlation coefficients, he suggested ρ = .1, .3, .5. These standards are based on his experience in dealing with the issues of critical effect sizes and remain reasonable standards today. However, Cohen warned against reifying these standards, reminding users that the standards do change in different specific situations, a warning that has not always been well heeded.

1.7 Power

To recap: From the exploration, we have a specific research hypothesis with theoretical rationale and empirical justification and some assurance that proving such a hypothesis would be of clinical and practical importance. For that hypothesis, we have the definition of a population effect size, which is 0 or less when the null hypothesis is true (our hypothesis untrue) and increasing the more true and important our hypothesis is. We propose a test that is a valid statistical test at the α-level (usually the 5% level), which means that when the effect size is zero or less (consistent with the null hypothesis), the probability that the test will lead to rejection of the null hypothesis is less than α (usually .05).

The *power* of a test for any effect size greater than zero (when the null hypothesis is false and our hypothesis true) is the probability that the test will lead to rejection of the null hypothesis, thus providing support for our theory. Generally, if that effect size is positive but very close to zero, the power of a valid 5% level test is just slightly greater than α (say 5%). The larger the effect size, the greater the power, and with a large enough effect size, the power will approach 100%. What is the power of a valid 5% level test? The quick answer: The power of any 5%-level statistical test is any number between 5% and 100%, depending on what the true effect size is.

Consequently, it is a foolish (or at least an incompletely stated) question to ask what the power of an α-level test is. The appropriate question is whether the test is *adequately powered* or not. To be adequately powered, the power of a test should be above some prespecified level (conventional levels: 70% or 80%) for any population effect size greater than the critical effect size.

Figure 1.7.1 shows the performance curves for the one-tailed and two-tailed 5% level t-tests, that is, the probability of rejecting the null hypothesis

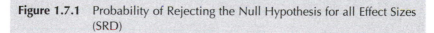

Figure 1.7.1   Probability of Rejecting the Null Hypothesis for all Effect Sizes (SRD)

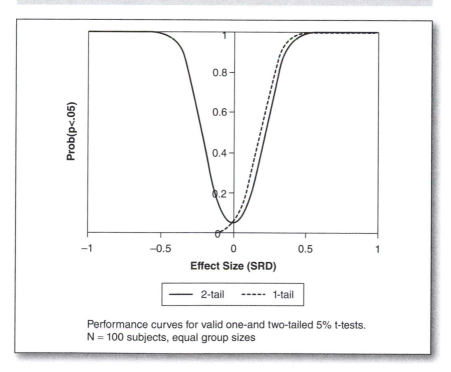

Performance curves for valid one-and two-tailed 5% t-tests.
N = 100 subjects, equal group sizes

for every possible value of the population effect size, here SRD. Every valid test has some such performance curve. Note that for the one-tailed test, the probability is at or below 5% for all SRD less than or equal to zero, and that for the two-tailed test, the probability is at 5% for SRD equal zero—showing that these are indeed valid 5% level tests. For both tests, as one moves away from SRDs consistent with the null hypothesis (SRD > 0 for the one-tailed test, and SRD ≠ 0 for the two-tailed test), the probability increases.

In Figure 1.7.2 are shown four different valid 5% level one-tailed tests: the one-tailed two sample t-test and three tests used when the outcome measure used in the two-sample t-test are dichotomized, at the midpoint between the two sample means and at 1 and 1.5 standard deviations above that midpoint. Also indicated is the critical effect size, SRD*, here set at what Cohen called a "medium" effect size. All four of these tests are valid to test the one-tailed hypothesis that A > B at the 5% significance level, but if one were to choose which to use, the choice would obviously be the t-test because it gives the greatest power. If the preset criterion for adequate power were 80% to detect any SRD greater than the critical effect size SRD*, the t-test here would be the only choice.

Figure 1.7.2   Reduction in Statistical Power Using Three Methods of Dichotomization

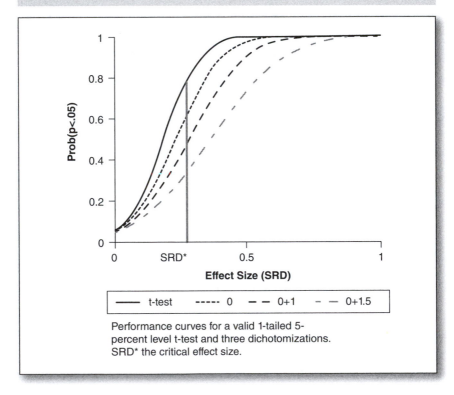

Performance curves for a valid 1-tailed 5-percent level t-test and three dichotomizations. SRD* the critical effect size.

Later we will discuss many different tests and strategies to increase power, either by increasing sample size or without increasing sample size; by changing design features; choosing better measures of outcomes; and so forth. However, all we want to emphasize now is that the one and only point at which the question *How Many Subjects?* has any relevance in the scientific method is this one step, that of designing a hypothesis-testing study. However, success at this step presupposes prior exploration activities, and the success of performing this step depends on following through with the rest of the process. Let us complete that cycle before we focus on this step in the process.

PILOT STUDY

A pilot study is a feasibility study done in preparation for a hypothesis testing study. Such studies are essential to the success of the hypothesis testing studies. Unfortunately, as we have noted earlier, the term pilot study is often misused to cover poorly designed studies with small sample sizes, a better definition is, a study (usually a small study) done to demonstrate the feasibility *of the design decided upon in the previous step for a hypothesis-testing study*. There are often aspects of that design that researchers are not sure can be implemented in the milieu in which the study is to be done, whether those aspects are the best choice.

For example, the design proposes to sample 100 patients per year for three years—but are there 100 per year available to be sampled? The design proposes that each patient complete a battery of tests in a four-hour period. But can that whole battery be completed in a four-hour period? The design proposes a certain outcome as the primary outcome, but there are several different instruments available to measure that outcome. Which of those, for the population to be sampled, is most reliable and valid? Which is likely to provide the clearest picture of what is actually happening? Any such questions had better be answered before the hypothesis-testing study is started. Thus, if the question is the availability of 100 subjects per year, one might propose to spend some time and effort to go through clinic records for the past several years, identifying who would be eligible for the study and making a reasonable guess as to how many of those would be willing to participate. Even better might be to briefly contact a sample of those eligible patients, explain what study is being proposed, and ask whether they would have been willing to participate had they been asked to do so. A tongue-in-cheek rule often attributed to Louis Lasagna (an eminent medical researcher known for his revision of the Hippocratic Oath) says that in designing a clinical trial, take the number of patients you think will be eligible and willing in the time period of interest and cut that by half, and that will probably exceed the number you will have available to you. Others have wryly suggested that the best way to cure a disease is to do a randomized clinical trial of treatments for the disease. Suddenly, there are few with the disease to be recruited! In short, researchers have long had the experience of beginning a well-designed, adequately powered research study only to find that the required number of subjects is simply not available, and the study subsequently fails. It is far better to know your limits before the study begins.

What if you don't and find out, after the study is proposed and funded and some number of patients are recruited and put through the study protocol, that some design feature can't be implemented? Only half the subjects planned for will be available. Or the battery that should have taken four hours actually takes eight, with many patients unwilling to return a second day to complete the battery. Or the battery actually does take four hours, but by the end of that time, both participant and assessor are so fatigued that there are serious questions about the validity and reliability of information in the latter portion of the battery. Or patients refused to cooperate in yielding the outcome measure selected. None of these scenarios are unknown or rare. If the study continues, whether as planned or with protocol modifications during the course of the study, chances are very good that the study will fail.

Consider this true story: Halfway through the research study, a paper appeared pointing out the deficiencies of the outcome measure being used in the research study and proposing a new measure said to be more valid and reliable and more sensitive to individual differences among the patients in the outcome of interest. The researchers proposed to switch from the old measure to the new at a point during the study when about a third of the patients had been assessed only with the old measure, another third had had their initial assessments with the old measure and, at some point in their follow-up, would be switched to the new measure. The final third of patients would be assessed only with the new measure. The researchers felt that the only way their results could ultimately be credible would be to make such a switch, but the statisticians, concerned about validity and power, objected.

The statisticians argued that the entire study should be completed, as proposed, with the old measure—after all, the rationale and justification of the proposal for the study was based on the old measure, not the new one. Alternatively the two-thirds of the patients done wholly or partially with the old measure should be set aside, and the study should be restarted with the new measure. But then the researchers would have had to recruit additional patients into the study to replace the ones set aside in order to have an adequate sample size, without adequate resources available to do so. Moreover, there were ethical considerations. After recruiting those patients into a research study, placing the burden of participation on patients already coping with medical problems, would it not be unethical simply to set their data aside and not use it at all?

A compromise was reached: The study would be completed with the new measure, as the researchers insisted, but the next 30 assessments were to be done using both the old and the new measures in random order. The statisticians could then assess the association between the two measures and set up a new analysis plan that accounted for the switch in measures. This change would cost some power but would (partially) satisfy both researchers and statisticians. However, the statisticians found that the correlation between the two measures was essentially zero! Both measures had been shown to be reasonably reliable, so the results mean the old and new measures corresponded to totally different constructs. Throwing all the data into one study was the equivalent of measuring height for half the subjects and income for the other half—the classic "apples and oranges" problem. The study was completed using the new measure (and construct) and the study failed. In fact, both studies, that with the old measure and that with the new measure, each with about half the subject assessments, failed; both because of inadequate sample size.

It is not unusual that a major change in the design after the study begins will decrease both the validity and the power, thus making study failure more likely. It is far better to check any questionable aspects of the research design in a pilot study, before the hypothesis-testing study is begun, and then, whatever happens, keep to the original research protocol. Keeping to the original research protocol is often referred to as *fidelity*.

HYPOTHESIS TESTING (HT) EXECUTION

At this point, researchers have a strong and important hypothesis with rationale and justification from exploration, and they've designed a study using information from exploration, which is feasible (from the pilot study) and valid and adequately powered to test that hypothesis. Thus, if the null hypothesis is true, the chances of a false positive conclusion, one that seems to support an untrue hypothesis, is less than, say, 5%, and the chances of a true positive conclusion if the hypothesis is of clinical or practical importance (i.e., a true effect size greater than the critical value also determined from exploration) is greater than, say, 80%.

All that remains is to execute that study, as designed, that is, with *fidelity*. To statisticians, it is amazing how often this does not happen. Researchers will often reconsider their own decisions partway through the study, and will "tweak" the sampling, measurement, design, treatment protocols, and so forth. Any such tweaking is likely to compromise the validity and/or power of the study to test the original hypothesis. Even more dismaying is how often researchers look at the data and tweak their original hypothesis. Any test done on a hypothesis based on examining the data is post hoc testing. The *p*-values are then miscomputed, and the conclusions drawn from such testing are highly questionable. In one study, (Chan, Hrobjartsson, Haahar, Gotzsche, & Altman, 2004), comparison of the a priori hypothesis with what was tested in the randomized clinical trial indicated that fully 60% of the studies had either modified or changed their outcomes—very likely, post hoc hypotheses. This is probably one major factor why so many published research results are false (Ioannidis, 2004).

REPORTING THE RESULTS OF A HYPOTHESIS-TESTING STUDY

Now the hypothesis-testing study is completed as designed, and the proposed tests are done and the conclusions drawn. Chances are that, with a strong and important hypothesis, a strong and feasible design, a valid test, and adequate power, the results will be convincing and publishable. What should be reported in such a publication?

The hypothesis (hypotheses) should be clearly stated along with a brief summary of the rationale and justification for that hypothesis in the introductory section. The design needs to be completely, clearly, but concisely described in the Materials and Methods section, as should the choice of statistical test and documentation of its validity and adequate power, including a statement regarding the critical value of the effect size set a priori. What significance level and power requirement was set a priori should here be stated. In the Results section, information should be presented about the population(s) sampled so that readers can judge whether the results apply to populations of interest to them. There also the results of statistical testing are presented. It is not sufficient to report only the p-value. To show that $p < .05$ only means that the power was sufficient to document support for the hypothesis. However, even if the null hypothesis is true and especially if the theory is true but trivial, there is some chance of a false positive result. Consequently, one should also report the estimated population effect size and its confidence interval. If that estimated population effect size is below the a priori critical value, it should be noted that the effect, even if statistically significant, may not be of clinical or practical significance.

For the hypothesis that A ≠ B, there are six possible patterns of results, shown in Figure 1.7.3. Each line in Figure 1.7.3 is a 95% two-tailed confidence interval for the population SRD based on the sample, that is, there is a 95% probability that the interval covers the true effect size. Such a confidence interval is closely associated with a 5% two-tailed statistical test:

- If the confidence interval does not include SRD = 0, then the result is statistically significant at the 5% level (i.e., p < .05). Thus situations #1, #2, and #3 show statistically significant results.
- If the confidence interval does not include any SRDs below the critical value, then the result is both statistically and clinically significant: #1.
- If the confidence interval does not include any SRDs above the critical value, then the result is not clinically significant: #3, #4. Note, however, #3 is statistically significant (SRD = 0 is not included), while #4 is not.
- Finally if the confidence interval includes both zero and effect sizes above the critical value, the study has failed (#5, #6). Before the study was done, there was equipoise as to whether the hypothesis was true or not. For failed studies, that equipoise remains unshaken after the study results are in.

Figure 1.7.3   Reporting Statistical and Clinical Significance From Null
Hypothesis Testing

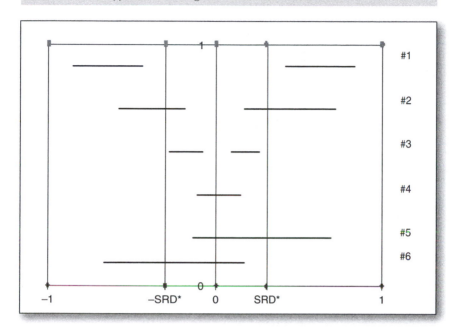

The length of the confidence interval is strongly connected with the power of the statistical test. Low power means very wide confidence intervals (like #5 and #6) and failed studies. High power means very tight confidence intervals that would establish either that the effect was of clinical and practical significance (#1) or of no clinical or practical significance (#3, #4). Moderate power is likely to support the hypothesis but not necessarily establish clinical significance (#2).

Many currently urge that every p-value be accompanied by an effect size with its confidence interval like those in Figure 1.7.3. Hypothesis-testing studies testing hypotheses with strong rationale and justification, and with designs and analyses that are valid and adequately powered, would more rapidly settle scientific questions and speed scientific progress.

It is highly recommended that when a study is published the data on which the conclusions of the study are based be shared with other researchers. This would not only broaden the evidence base available for further exploration for the next generation of studies but would allow others to check the internal validity of the results. If a mistake is made in the analysis, for example, a two-sample t-test is used when the assumptions are not met, it may be embarrassing to admit the mistake but far more embarrassing if that mistake were to mislead future research in the field.

INDEPENDENT REPLICATION/VALIDATION: SCIENTIFIC TRUTH

Finally, no scientific fact can be established by one research study, no matter how well conceived, well designed, well analyzed, and carefully reported. There should always be independent replication or validation of any conclusion before it is accepted as scientific fact. When independent studies are done that replicate or validate, the data from these studies should also be shared for the reasons mentioned above.

RETURN TO EXPLORATION

And so we return full-cycle to exploration (Figure 1.0). However, when we return, there should have been major progress. Not only is the information base available for exploration far greater, but conclusions would have been reached that change the state of knowledge. That should mean that hypotheses in the next generation should be broader, deeper, and even more important to scientific progress.

Anyone involved in research would likely scoff that this is the process used, and we would agree—what is here is ideal rather than actual. However, the closer researchers come to the ideal process, the more likely will be a rapid scientific progress. The greater the deviation from the ideal process, the greater is the chance of major errors, such as wasted time and resources in failed studies, non-reproducible findings, or slow progress.

REFERENCES

Acion, L., Peterson, J. J., Temple, S., & Arndt, S. (2006). Probabilistic index: An intuitive non-parametric approach to measuring the size of treatment effects. *Statistics in Medicine, 25*(4), 591–602.

Chan, A. W., Hrobjartsson, A., Haahr, M. T., Gotzsche, P. C., & Altman, D. G. (2004). Empirical evidence for selective reporting of outcome in randomized trials. *Journal of the American Medical Association, 291*(20), 2457–2465.

Cohen, J. (1988). *Statistical power analysis for the behavioral sciences.* Hillsdale, NJ: Lawrence Erlbaum.

Cooper, H., & Hedges, L. V. (1994). *The handbook of research synthesis.* New York: Russell Sage.

Cumming, G. (2012). *Understanding the new statistics: Effect sizes, confidence intervals, and meta-analysis.* New York: Routledge.

Ellis, P. D. (2010). *The essential guide to effect sizes*. New York: Cambridge University Press.

Freedman, B. (1987). Equipoise and the ethics of clinical research. *The New England Journal of Medicine, 317,* 141–145.

Grissom, R. J., & Kim, J. J. (2012). *Effect sizes for research: Univariate and multivariate applications*. New York: Routledge.

Ioannidis, J. P. A. (2005). Why most published research findings are false. *PLoS Medicine, 2*(8), 696–791.

Jones, D. R. (1995). Meta-analysis: Weighing the evidence. *Statistics in Medicine, 14,* 137–149.

Kraemer, H. C., & Kupfer, D. J. (2006). Size of treatment effects and their importance to clinical research and practice. *Biological Psychiatry, 59*(11), 990–996.

McGough, J. J., & Faraone, S. V. (2009). Estimating the size of treatment effects: Moving beyond *p* values. *Psychiatry (Edgmont), 6*(10), 21–29.

2

General Concepts

From this point on, the focus of attention is on that one step in the scientific method that is labeled Hypothesis Testing in Figure 1.0. The scientific method requires that the researchers proposing a theory (e.g., drinking coffee may affect health) put that theory to an empirical test. *Statistical hypothesis testing* is one such formalized empirical test, in structure analogous to the Anglo-Saxon system of trial by jury.

The basic overall principle is that the researchers' theory is considered false until demonstrated beyond reasonable doubt to be true. Until the evidence demonstrates the dangers or benefits of drinking coffee, we assume that drinking coffee makes no difference to health. This is expressed as an assumption that the *null hypothesis*, the contradiction of the researchers' theory, is true. Thus the null hypothesis is that drinking coffee makes no difference to health. What is considered a "reasonable" doubt is called the *significance level*. By convention in scientific research, a reasonable level of remaining doubt is one below either 5% or 1% probability.

The researchers evaluate the preliminary evidence (literature review, case histories, theoretical considerations, pilot studies, etc.) and decide whether or not the case is important enough and whether or not preliminary evidence is convincing enough to test the hypothesis (exploration).

The researchers also formulate the hypothesis testing strategy. They decide what design to use, which measure of response to use, the number and timing of measurements per subject, which test to use, and how many subjects to sample. All of these decisions affect how likely the evidence is to be "convincing beyond reasonable doubt"—the *power* of the study.

For example, in the coffee drinking study, we must somehow measure coffee drinking. We could do this by asking a retrospective self-report of each subject (e.g., "Normally, how many cups of coffee do you drink per day?"). Alternatively, we could ask each subject to keep a diary of coffee drinking for a week or two or we could directly monitor or measure coffee intake in some way.

Similarly, we could assess the health of the subjects by requiring a complete physical exam including Xrays and lab tests. We could do this once or every six months for 10 years. Or we could have a medical professional take a health history and inventory and do this once or periodically. Or we could use some self-report system such as the Cornell Medical Index* (Brodman et al., 1949) and do this once or periodically.

Clearly, using self-reports of coffee drinking and health only once (cross-sectional study) will be cheaper than using professional assessment or doing a longitudinal study. Which decisions we make will obviously affect how convincing the result will be and how costly and time-consuming the study.

A *statistical* test defines a rule that, when applied to the data, determines whether the null hypothesis can be rejected, that is, whether the evidence is convincing beyond reasonable doubt. Both the significance level and the power of the test are derived by calculating with what probability a positive verdict would be obtained (the null hypothesis rejected) if the same trial were run over and over again. To obtain the significance level, these hypothetical reruns are done when the null hypothesis is taken to be true and is the upper limit of that probability for various effect sizes consistent with the null hypothesis. To obtain power, these hypothetical reruns are done when the researchers' theory is true and the power is the lower limit of these probabilities for various effect sizes greater than the critical effect size. The student in an introductory course is, in most cases, given the rule (the statistical test) and (hopefully but not always) is told the circumstances in which the rule applies (the assumptions) but is not taught how to derive each test (how the reruns are actually done). Over the last century, various statisticians have developed a number of statistical tests, and they have done the calculations necessary to determine the significance level and power of such tests.

For a test to be a *valid* 5% or 1% test, the computation of significance level must be correct. Such computations involve certain assumptions about the nature of the population. If a certain test were used when the population did not meet these assumptions, the test may be *invalid*: a mistrial. Frequently, however, the test is derived under a number of specific assumptions, but only a few are crucial to the validity of the test. Tests having few assumptions crucial to their validity are known as *robust* tests.

For the computation of power, the researchers must have developed from the preliminary evidence a *critical effect size*, a measure of how strong the theory must minimally be to be of practical or clinical importance. So, for example, the very minimal increase a subject may have on the Cornell Medical Index is one point (on a 195-point scale). Previous evidence indicates that for every 10 years, the index increases about three to four points. The difference between a

---

*The Cornell Medical Index has not been used recently and is used here for illustrative purposes only.

healthy subject and one with an acute illness is about five to six points. With this as background information, how small an increase in the index would occasion social concerns about the safety of coffee drinking? Certainly no less than one point but perhaps as much as 10 points would be required to motivate social and economic recommendations for or against coffee drinking. Such background information is used to estimate a *critical effect size.*

Put another way: Suppose coffee drinking did harm health. If you could get people to stop drinking coffee, how many would avoid experiencing that harm. If the critical effect size is NNT = 1000, that means of every 1000 people who could be induced to quit drinking coffee, one less person would experience harm. If NNT = 10, one in every 10; if NNT = 2, one in every two. Now considering the burden placed on individuals, the impact on commerce, and so forth, how small must NNT be to seriously consider a ban on coffee drinking. If that NNT = 10, that is the critical effect size.

Such specification of the critical effect size is based on the researchers' understanding and knowledge of their field, supplemented by the preliminary evidence available, and reflects both population characteristics and the proposed research design. It is important to realize that one cannot plan a cost-effective study without any background or preliminary information—any more than a prosecutor would institute a trial by jury without evidence to back the charge.

Changing designs, changing the measure to be used, or choosing one valid test rather than another changes the definition of the effect size. Furthermore, the critical effect size is population specific as well as measurement specific. What the critical effect size is for 20-year-old men might be very different from that for 50-year-old women. What the critical effect size will be using the CMI might be very different from using another health index or a score generated from a physician's report. The researchers may well consider different designs and measures before deciding on the final proposal for the trial. They would then choose the strategy that seems most powerful or one that has sufficient power but is least costly.

Researchers should remember several points. There is a difference between preliminary evidence and the trial itself. One cannot formulate a theory by examining some evidence and then test it on the same material (post hoc testing). Preliminary evidence is meant to convince the researchers that a trial is worthwhile, but the trial must be run on a hypothesis that is stated a priori.

Also, the question of power enters consideration only in planning a study, not after the study is done and the verdict is in. If the verdict is negative, that is, a nonsignificant or nonconvincing result, then the researchers' theory was inadequate or their evaluation of preliminary evidence was faulty or their design, measurement, analysis, or sample-size decisions were flawed. In short, somewhere along the line, decisions were inadequate. One might well use the evidence of this trial as preliminary evidence in planning a better future trial, but no post hoc power calculations change the outcome of this trial. There is some flavor of double jeopardy in a researchers' report that, although result of trial is negative (a nonsignificant result), the "trend" was in the right direction and supported the researchers' theory.

On the other hand, if the verdict is positive, the decisions were willy-nilly good enough. (Moses's Principle of the Blunt Ax quoted by Goldstein: "If the ax chopped down the tree, it was sharp enough" (1964, p. 62).) However, the question then is what to make of that chopped-down tree. What is the estimated effect size and its confidence interval? Is the estimated effect size estimated precisely enough to draw a conclusion as to whether or not the effect is of practical or clinical significance? If it is, comparison of the estimated effect size and the critical effect size will determine that conclusion.

2.1 Introduction to the Power Table

The master table at the end of the text contains four sections corresponding to one- and two-tailed 5% and 1% tests of significance. The 5% and 1% are the most commonly used levels of significance. As a reminder, whether the test is one or two tailed is determined by how the researchers' theory is formulated. In our mock trial, the theory states that drinking coffee affects health, leaving the direction unspecified—a two-tailed theory. This is because exploration indicates some evidence of harm from coffee drinking and other evidence of benefit. It is quite possible that the evidence in a future study could go in either direction—neither is precluded by exploration. Thus a one-tailed theory would here be inappropriate. If the situation had been different and there were no indication of any benefit from drinking coffee, the theory would have been one-tailed. It is important to note that the choice between a one-tailed and two-tailed test is determined not only by which direction the researchers think or hope the results will support but by whether one direction is illogical or already precluded by the evidence in previous research.

The columns of each section of the table relate to various levels of power (10% to 99%) or the probability of obtaining a significant result (i.e., rejecting the null hypothesis) for the statistical test. In the trial by jury analogy, power is the likelihood of a guilty verdict. The rows relate to an index, Δ, that is determined by which statistical test is to be used, by the critical effect size based on the researcher's knowledge of the field, and from preliminary evidence as well as, sometimes, by certain design features (e.g., the balance in sample size between two groups being compared). The index Δ has values ranging from 0 to 1. A value of 0 (or less) means that the researchers' theory is false. A value of 1.00 is an "open and shut case." The index Δ lies somewhere between these extremes and reflects design and population parameters but not the sample size.

In the body of the table, numbers designated v are listed. These numbers correspond to sample size in ways determined by the design of the study but do not involve any population parameters.

A "population parameter" is some numerical characteristic of the population (mean, variance, etc.), which is unknown and is to be estimated using a sample from the population. A "design parameter" reflects the choice of the researcher, for example, as to how to allocate subjects to groups (equal numbers) or how many observations per subject to take (1, 2, . . .) and the spacing or circumstances of these observations (every 6 months, every year, after 10 years). The most important design parameter is the sample size, the total number of subjects sampled from the population (s) who will participate in the study.

Once the researchers identify which test is to be used, instructions will be provided to compute Δ and v in terms of the design and population parameters. With these, one can use the appropriate section of the master table by specifying any two of the three entries (i.e., power, critical effect size, and sample size) and reading off the third.

For practice at this stage, regard v as the sample size and follow these exercises:

- To have 90% power for a 5% one-tailed test with a critical effect size of $\Delta = 0.4$, one would need 49 (v) subjects.
- If the test were to be a two-tailed 5% test, one would need 60 subjects.
- For one- and two-tailed 1% tests, the numbers would be 74 and 84.
- If the effect were smaller, say $\Delta = 0.10$, these numbers would not be 49, 60, 74, and 84 but would be 852, 1045, 1295, and 1480.
- If one were satisfied to have 80% chance of success, the number would be 36 for a one-tailed 5% test with a critical effect size of $\Delta = 0.4$ and 616 with a critical effect size of $\Delta = 0.1$.

It is a good idea to play around with these tables just to familiarize yourself with the way the table is structured.

From such exercises, we can learn several "facts of life":

- The more stringent the significance level, the greater the necessary sample size. More subjects are needed for a 1% level test than for a 5% level test for the same effect size.
- Two-tailed tests require larger sample sizes than one-tailed tests. Logically, assessing two directions at the same time requires a somewhat greater investment in effort.
- The smaller the critical effect size, the larger the necessary sample size. Subtle effects require greater efforts.
- The larger the power required, the larger the necessary sample size. Greater protection from failure requires greater effort.

- The smaller the sample size, the smaller the power, that is, the greater the chance of failure (a hung jury or a not-guilty verdict).
- If one proposed to go to trial with a sample size of 20 or fewer subjects, one must be willing to take a high risk of failure or be operating in an area in which the critical effect size is large indeed.

The late statistician James Boen told an amusing story that illustrates a type of problem common here. A researcher came to him asking, *How Many Subjects?* in this case, mice, to test a certain theory. She agreed that a 5% significance level with a two-tailed test was appropriate in her field, and they both agreed on which test to use. "What sort of effect is critical here?" he asked. She said that, in her field, even quite a small effect size would be critical. He explained what the effect size meant and explained $\Delta = .1$, which in any statistician's experience would be very, very small.

"Oh no," she said. "Effect sizes much smaller would be important."

He asked what she had in mind: $\Delta = .08$? .06? .02? .01?

Finally she agreed to $\Delta = .01$, and he asked her how much power she required.

"Ah," she said. "I really can't tolerate much chance of failure—let's say, 99% power."

"Then you're going to need 183,714 mice."

"Are you crazy?" She stomped out of his office.

A few days later, Jim ran into her in the coffee room and asked what she had decided to do and she said she figured 30 mice should do it!

Consider what happened here. For a two-tailed 5%-level test, to detect a moderate effect size ($\Delta = .24$), 30 subjects give her about 25% power. In short, if she was right in her initial arguments and the critical effect size was much lower than that, her chance of detecting it was almost nil, and the study was very likely to fail.

To achieve 99% power for a critical effect size of 0.01 (as she and most students initially specify), a researcher must be prepared to recruit and process more than 150,000 subjects. The acid test of whether an effect size of 0.01 is, in fact, "important to society" is whether society is prepared to fund a study requiring 150,000 subjects and the researchers willing to recruit and process that number. Specification of the critical effect size and the required power, we can only repeat, must be realistic, not idealistic.

In the master table, no values of v are listed that are less than 10—a personal bias of the authors. At a meeting of statisticians, all experienced in biomedical research, someone once asked whether we had a minimal number, some sample size below which we would not be willing to undertake a study. There was quite a range of answers, from 10 to 100. This wasn't a question about power but a question as to whether some sample sizes are too small to even consider wasting time on. Moreover, the minimum sample size necessary for the credibility of a study differs from field to field. Seldom is an opinion survey done with fewer than 1,000 subjects. Sociological studies and epidemiological studies rarely use fewer than several hundred subjects. Clinical trials in medicine with 10 to 20 subjects per group are sometimes seen, but generally successful such trials have 100 or more subjects. A clinical trial testing the effectiveness of a vaccine against a relatively rare disorder (polio, AIDS) might need 10,000 subjects. In some areas of behavioral research, published peer-reviewed studies can be based on a sample size of one. Such differences in the minimum acceptable sample size reflect the types of questions, designs, measures, and analyses that are used in a particular field and therefore the sample sizes necessary for reasonable power. To some extent, what one views as an "appropriate" sample size reflects what is customary in a field, or is developed from personal past experience. The decision to list no sample sizes less than 10 in Table 1, however, is due not so much to what researchers consider an adequate sample size for publication but to a concern about the accuracy of power calculations when sample sizes are too small, although in our case, we would not be willing to waste time on a study with fewer than 10 per group.

2.2 Statistical Considerations

An important question is whether it is, in fact, possible to compile a single table appropriate for a wide selection of common statistical tests. Chapter 3 includes explanations and derivations (for the one-tailed tests) of the master table. The derivations may not be of interest to nonstatistical researchers and is designed so that it might be skipped without compromising the understanding of what follows.

However, a few key points should be noted. The values of v in the master table should be regarded as approximate. In fact, for certain tests (intraclass correlation, homogeneity of variance with balanced independent samples), the results are exact under the assumptions on which the tests are based. For others (correlation coefficients, t-tests) they are likely to be very accurate, for they are based on approximation procedures known to be very accurate (Boomsma, 1977; Chaubey & Mudholkar, 1978; Kraemer, 1975). However, in general, it is better policy to *always* regard them as approximations. First, in many cases they *are* approximations and not the best of all available ones. Second, in practice we will use linear or even "eye-ball" interpolation in the tables. This compromises accuracy even for the exact results. Third and most important, it is seldom known with certainty that the assumptions underlying the test are precisely met. Finally, as we have seen, the critical effect size is itself only an estimate. At best, the results can only be as accurate as the estimates and assumptions are true.

In Chapters 4 through 9, we demonstrate power calculations for a variety of different statistical tests. In every case, we first describe the critical effect size for the test (Δ), that minimum effect considered important to detect, using information from exploration to estimate its magnitude. We also demonstrate how the v from the master table relates to the sample size our test requires. The summary table provides a convenient summary of these results for a number of common tests.

REFERENCES

Boomsma, A. (1977). Comparing approximations of confidence intervals for the product-moment correlation coefficient. *Statistica Neerlandica, 31,* 179–185.

Brodman, K., Erdman, A., Lorge, I., & Wolfe, H. (1949). The Cornell Medical Index: An adjunct to medical interview. *JAMA, 140*(6), 530–534.

Chaubey, Y. P., & Mudholkar, G. S. (1978). A new approximation for Fisher's Z. *Australian Journal of Statistics, 20,* 250–256.

Goldstein, A. (1964). *Biostatistics: An introductory text.* New York: McMillan.

Kraemer, H. C. (1975). On estimation and hypothesis testing problems for correlation coefficients. *Psychometrika, 40*(4), 473–485.

3

The Pivotal Case: Intraclass Correlation

Behind every statistical test is some statisticians' work that specified the assumptions, developed the distribution theory, formulated the one- or two-tailed test at the α-level, and developed the theoretical basis of power calculations for that test. Generally, users of the tests are completely unaware of this statistical background, trusting that the work done has been vetted by other statisticians and proven to be correct. No objections to that—after some years, most statisticians would have a hard time quickly recalling exactly how the distribution theory of the t-test or the correlation coefficient was derived. The discussion in this chapter is not meant to entice users of statistical tests to become adept at deriving test theory. It is written for two purposes. First, for those users curious to see the process at least once in order to have some awareness of what this work entails, this discussion might be of some interest. Second, it is important to document for statistical readers exactly how the tables that will be used for power computations were developed and organized.

3.1 An Intraclass Correlation Test

Suppose (X_i, Y_i), $i = 1, 2, \ldots n$, are drawn from a bivariate normal population with population correlation coefficient ρ and equal variances. The maximum likelihood estimate of ρ is the intraclass correlation coefficient (r_I) (Kraemer, 1975) where

$$r_I = \frac{2\Sigma\left(x_i - \bar{x}\right)\left(y_i - \bar{y}\right)}{\sqrt{\Sigma\left(x_i - \bar{x}\right)^2 + \Sigma\left(y_i - \bar{y}\right)^2}} .$$

Whatever the value of ρ,

$$u = u(r_I, \rho) = (r_I - \rho)/(1 - r_I \rho) \tag{3.1.1}$$

has a distribution that depends only on $v = n - 1$, specifically,

$$v^{1/2} u/(1 - u^2)^{1/2} \sim t_\upsilon , \tag{3.1.2}$$

the t-distribution with v degrees of freedom. The percentile points of the u-distribution (3.1.2) are easily computed from the percentile points of the t-distribution:

$$u_{v\alpha} = t_{v\alpha} / (t_{v\alpha}^2 + v)^{1/2} . \tag{3.1.3}$$

These values are tabled and readily available, as Pearson and Hartley show (1962, p. 138, Table 13).

A simple choice for the population effect size is simply ρ, and the estimated effect size after the study is done is r_I.

To test the null hypothesis H_0: $\rho \leq 0$ vs. A: $\rho > 0$, one would reject H_0 at the α level if

$$u(r_I, 0) = r_I \geq u_{v\alpha}. \tag{3.1.4}$$

The power of this test (P) at any critical effect size $\rho > 0$ is the solution to the equation (Kraemer, 1975)

$$\Delta = (u_{v\alpha} - u_{vP})/(1 - u_{v\alpha} u_{vP}), \tag{3.1.5}$$

where

$$\Delta = \rho.$$

The master table presents the exact solution to (3.1.5) (v rounded to the next higher integer value) and therefore to any problem concerning power, the solution to which depends on a distribution, such as that specified in (3.1.1) and (3.1.2).

3.2 The ANOVA Approach to the Intraclass Correlation Test

Let us now look at this same problem somewhat differently. It is known that the computation of this intraclass correlation coefficient may be based on the Two-Way (subjects × 2 tests) Analysis of Variance (ANOVA); for examples, see Bartko (1976) and Haggard (1958). The F-test for subjects in this analysis, $\hat{F}$, can be shown to be

$$\hat{F} = (1 + r_I)/(1 - r_I). \tag{3.2.1}$$

From ANOVA theory (subjects a random effect)

$$\hat{F} \sim \lambda F_{v,v}, \quad \lambda = (1 + \rho)/(1 - \rho). \tag{3.2.2}$$

Testing H_0: $\rho \le 0$ vs. A: $\rho > 0$ is absolutely equivalent to testing H_0: $\lambda \le 1$ vs. A: $\lambda > 1$. The test based on $\hat{F}$ is exactly equivalent to that based on r_I.

What this means is that for any test of H_0: $\lambda \le 1$ vs. A: $\lambda > 1$, based on a statistic $\hat{F}$ having the distribution described in (3.2.2), one can compute $v = n - 1$ and $\Delta = (\lambda - 1)/(\lambda + 1)$ and use the master table to execute exact power calculations.

3.3 Normal Approximation to the Intraclass Theory

Let us look at this problem in yet a third way. From (3.2.2),

$$0.5 \ \ln[(1 + r_I)/(1 - r_I)] \sim 0.5 \ \ln[(1 + \rho)/(1 - \rho)] + 0.5 \ \ln F_{v,v}. \tag{3.3.1}$$

The transformation $Z(r) = 0.5 \ln[(1 + r)/(1 - r)]$ is well known as Fisher's transformation of the correlation coefficient (Fisher, 1921). The random variable $0.5 \ln F_{v,v}$ has approximately a normal distribution with mean 0 and variance $1/(h - 1)$ where h is the harmonic mean of the two degrees of freedom (Fisher & Yates, 1957). Here $h = n - 1$.

Again, what this means is that for any test of H_0: $Z(\Delta) \le 0$ vs. A: $Z(\Delta) > 0$ based on a statistic Z such that

$$Z \sim N(Z(\Delta), 1/N), \tag{3.3.2}$$

where N depends in some way on v. One can compute $v = N + 1$ and Δ and use the master table to execute approximate power calculations.

The case of the intraclass correlation coefficient is pivotal, for it furnishes a link between test of correlation coefficients, of variance ratios, and of mean differences. These are the three general problems that underlie most of the common test procedures introduced in an elementary statistical course.

3.4 Noncentral t

Now suppose one had a situation in which one wished to test the hypothesis $H_0 : \delta \leq 0$ vs. $A : \delta > 0$ using a test statistic T such that

$$T \sim t_v'(\sqrt{N\delta}),\tag{3.4.1}$$

where t is the noncentral t-distribution with v degrees of freedom and noncentrality parameter $\sqrt{N\delta}$. It is known that

$$T/(T^2 + v)^{1/2}\tag{3.4.2}$$

is approximately distributed as is the intraclass correlation coefficient (Kraemer & Paik, 1979) with

$$\rho = N^{1/2}\delta/(N\delta^2 + v)^{1/2} = \delta/(\delta^2 + v/N)^{1/2} \approx \delta/(\delta^2 + d)^{1/2}.\tag{3.4.3}$$

If δ and $d = v/N$ depended only on population and design parameters, then one could use the master table with

$$\Delta = \delta/(\delta^2 + d)^{1/2}.\tag{3.4.4}$$

3.5 Variance Ratios

Suppose one had a situation in which one wished to test the hypothesis $H_0 : \lambda \leq 1$ vs. $A : \lambda > 1$ using a test statistic $\hat{F}$ such that

$$\hat{F} \sim \lambda F_{v_1, v_2}\tag{3.5.1}$$

where v_1, v_2 depend only on sample size and design and λ on population characteristics and on design. If v_1 and v_2 were not too disparate or provided both were large, this distribution could be approximated by

$$\hat{F} \sim \lambda F_{h,h}, \tag{3.5.2}$$

where h is the harmonic mean of v_1 and v_2 (Fisher & Yates, 1957). Now one could use the master table with

$$v = h, \Delta = (\lambda - 1)/(\lambda + 1). \tag{3.5.3}$$

3.6 Discussion

Since many of the most commonly used tests are based either on the distribution theory of the correlation coefficient, normal distributions, the t-distribution, the chi-square distribution, or the F-distribution, what we have done is to provide a common basis for power computations. These computations are approximate—but all such computations are approximations—since we seldom know that the assumptions made are exactly correct or that the critical effect size reflects a universal opinion. Most approaches to power computations deal separately with these various distributions. However, when the problem is to compare the power of several different approaches, lack of easy translation from one possible valid test to another, where each test calls upon different effect sizes and/or different theoretical approaches, creates what are often impossible barriers to correct decision making. In such cases, this approach may be found the most appealing and useful.

REFERENCES

Bartko, J. J. (1976). On various intraclass correlation reliability coefficients. *Psychological Bulletin, 83*, 762–765.

Fisher, R. A. (1921). On the "probable error" of a coefficient of correlation deduced from a small sample. *Metron, 1*, 1–32.

Fisher, R. A., & Yates, F. (1957). *Statistical tables for biological, agricultural and medical research*. London: Oliver and Boyd.

Haggard, E. A. (1958). *Intraclass correlation and the analysis of variance*. New York: Dryden Press.

Kraemer, H. C. (1975). On estimation and hypothesis testing problems for correlation coefficients. *Psychometrika, 40*(4), 473–485.

Kraemer, H. C., & Paik, M. A. (1979). A central t approximation to the noncentral t-distribution. *Technometrics, 21*(3), 357–360.

Pearson, E. S., & Hartley, H. O. (1962). *Biometric tables for statisticians* (Vol. I). London: Cambridge University Press.

4

Equality of Means: z- and t-tests, Balanced ANOVA

T he sample mean is probably the most familiar of all statistical estimates. Tests of the corresponding population mean are usually the first ones taught in an elementary statistics course. These tests cover a wide variety of situations, corresponding to the many ways in which a researcher might choose to investigate the level of a variable in one or more populations.

4.1 Single-Sample Test, Variance Known: z-test

If the responses in the population of interest were known to be normally distributed with unknown mean μ and *known* variance σ^2, we might propose to reject the null hypothesis $H_0 : \mu = \mu_0$ if the quantity $(\bar{X} - \mu_0)/\sigma$, where $\bar{X}$ is the observed sample mean and μ_0 is a specified value (often zero), is greater than the $100(1 - \alpha)$th percentile of the standard normal distribution (one-tailed test) or if its absolute value is greater than the $100(1 - \alpha/2)$th percentile of that distribution (two-tailed test). These percentiles are available in most elementary statistical textbooks and in all statistical packages. This is the familiar z-test, often the first test discussed in an elementary statistics course. Here, the usual population effect size is δ, a version of Cohen's delta, where μ_0 is the value specified in the hypothesis to be tested (often zero) and σ^2 is the known variance:

$$\delta = (\mu - \mu_0) / \sigma. \tag{4.1.1}$$

To use the master tables to determine the sample size (n) needed to have the desired power, one would access the 5% or 1% one-tailed or two-tailed table (as determined by the specific hypothesis) and then locate the column with the desired power where the row is determined by

$$\Delta = (e^{2\delta} - 1)/(e^{2\delta} + 1).$$

Then the necessary sample is determined by the ν in the table as

$$\nu = n + 1.$$

Let's take an example. From exploratory studies, it appears that moderate coffee drinking (say three to five cups per day on self-report) may affect health, as indicated by a score on the Cornell Medical Index (Gordon, Emerson, & Simpson, 1959). In times past, it was thought that coffee drinking could not possibly be good for health, but in recent years, some evidence has appeared suggesting that non-excessive coffee drinking might actually be beneficial. Thus we propose a two-tailed test and a 5% significance level. We propose to take a sample of n men in their forties who are moderate coffee drinkers and assess their CMI.

From earlier studies using the CMI, it appears that healthy men in their forties have a CMI with mean about eight and standard deviation about 7 ($\mu_0 = 8$, $\sigma = 7$). If those in the moderate coffee drinking population sampled were to have a population mean (unknown μ) much different from $\mu_0 = 8$, it would suggest some association between coffee drinking and health. Note that we are not suggesting a causal association. Coffee drinking may be a marker for a whole complex of personal characteristics that may affect health, but showing that coffee drinking is a marker and the direction it takes (health benefit or harm) might motivate the more complicated and more difficult kinds of studies that would establish causality that, in turn, might influence medical policies.

That leads us to propose the null hypothesis that the unknown population mean μ is different from $\mu_0 = 8$. Moreover, let us suppose that we have documentation in the literature that changing the mean would not change the variance, and thus we know that $\sigma = 7$ in the population to be sampled. Our population effect size then is $\delta = (\mu - 8)/7$, μ unknown, an indication of how much of the population sampled lies above rather than below eight.

Let's pause here for a moment. It is to be noted that any monotonic function of δ is here also an effect size. For example, $\Delta = (e^{2\delta} - 1)/ (e^{2\delta} + 1)$ is also a population effect size here, the effect size that will be used in the master tables. Like δ, it has the value zero when the null hypothesis ($\mu_0 = 8$) is true and increases in magnitude the further above or below 8 the true value is. It has one (and, as far as we can tell, only one) advantage over δ; it ranges from -1 to $+1$, while δ theoretically, at least, ranges from $-\infty$ to $+\infty$. It is sometimes easier to evaluate the clinical or practical impact of an effect size with a finite range than one with infinite range. However, both δ and Δ are clearly interpretable only if the distribution of responses is normal with standard deviation seven as assumed. Interpretability is crucial when setting the critical effect size.

To ease this process, let us try another alternative effect size: SRD = Probability$(X > \mu_0)$ − Probability$(X < \mu_0)$, that is, a direct measure of how much weight of the distribution of X is above versus below μ_0 (here 8). That might be a great deal easier to interpret. Mathematically if the normal distribution and variance assumptions are true, then SRD = 2Φ (δ) − 1, where $\Phi()$ is the standard normal distribution. The particular advantage of SRD is that it is meaningful whatever the distribution of X is, normally distributed or not, and whatever the variance of X is, known or unknown, while the interpretation of δ or Δ, as defined here, depends on both those assumptions.

But clearly, which effect size researchers might choose to use to set the critical effect size in designing the study or to report in the results of their study is their choice. Anyone who disagrees can transform what is reported to what they prefer. Whichever effect size registers on a scale comfortable to understand is acceptable. In Table 4.1.1, we show the magnitudes of Δ (here with σ unknown and SRD for values of δ, when the assumptions for the single-sample designs are true).

Now for the critical effect size: From exploratory research, we know that the CMI tends to increase three to four points (say 3.5 points) for each 10 years of age. What would be an important enough difference to warrant clinical action? A one-point difference (on the 195-point CMI scale) would be minimal and probably not enough to warrant taking any public health action to reduce coffee drinking. But a 3.5-point difference corresponding to "aging" participants in terms of their CMI about 10 years would surely warrant clinical attention. Perhaps we can agree that a 3.5-point difference is critical, in which case the critical effect size is $\delta^* = 3.5/7 = 0.5$. That would correspond to a critical value on the Δ scale of .46 (which is used in the master tables), on the SRD scale of .38.

Cohen in his landmark book on power analysis (1988) suggested that δ^* = .2, .5, .8 correspond to "small," "medium," and "large" effect sizes, and it is remarkable how well this corresponds to the decisions at which researchers arrive. However, Cohen also warns that these standards not be reified; the critical effect size needs to be carefully considered in each context of research.

For a two-tailed test at the 5% level (see that table in the master tables) with 90% power (which locates the appropriate column in that table), for a critical effect size on the Δ scale of .46 (which locates the appropriate row in that table), we read $\nu = 44$ (interpolating between 46 and 36). Since $n = \nu-1$, the necessary sample size would be 43. For a 5% two-tailed test with 99% power, $\nu = 76$ (between 80 and 62), and thus the sample size would be 75.

Table 4.1.1   For the Single-Sample z-test (σ known) and for the Single-Sample t-test (σ unknown), the Values of Δ and SRD Corresponding to Values of Cohen's d (δ)

δ	Δ (σ unknown)	SRD	Δ (σ known)
0.0	0.00	0.00	0.00
0.1	0.10	0.08	0.10
0.2	0.20	0.16	0.20
0.3	0.29	0.24	0.29
0.4	0.38	0.31	0.37
0.5	0.46	0.38	0.45
0.6	0.54	0.45	0.51
0.7	0.60	0.52	0.57
0.8	0.66	0.58	0.62
0.9	0.72	0.63	0.67
1.0	0.76	0.68	0.71
1.5	0.91	0.87	0.83
2.0	0.96	0.95	0.89
2.5	0.99	0.99	0.93
3.0	1.00	1.00	0.95
∞	1.00	1.00	1.00

To familiarize yourself with the structure and use of the master tables, it would be worth playing around a little. What if we chose to use a one-tailed test at the 5% level? What if we used a 1% level instead for either the one- or two-tailed tests? What if we required 70% or 80% power rather than 90% or 99%? What if we set the critical effect size somewhat larger or somewhat smaller? What would the sample sizes then be?

From such warm-up exercises, certain general truths will emerge:

- The smaller the critical value, the larger the sample size must be. Moreover the association between critical value and sample size (other things equal) is far from linear. Very small critical values require enormous sample sizes.

- The more power required, the larger the sample size must be. Moreover, the association between required power level and sample size (other things equal) too is far from linear. The increase in sample size to move from 50% to 60% power is trivial compared to that to move from 89% to 99% power.
- It always takes a larger sample size for a two-tailed than for a one-tailed test.
- It always takes a larger sample size for a 1% than for a 5% significance level test.

The single-sample z-test is the one case when doing *exact* power calculations for the one-tailed test is as easy as using the tabled values. For an α-level test, with power P, the exact sample size necessary to detect a value of δ^* is $n = (Z_\alpha - Z_p)^2/\delta^{*2}$, where Z_α and Z_p are respectively the $1 - \alpha$ and $1 - P$ percentiles of the standard normal distribution, and δ^* is the critical value. In Table 4.1.2 appear the exact values of n and the values obtained by linear interpolation in the master table for a 5% one-tailed test, for 90% and 99% power. Generally, as here, there are minor differences in the recommended sample sizes between the sample sizes derived from exact calculations and from use of the master tables. Once again, remember that power calculations (even those based on exact calculations) yield approximations, not exact values, for sample sizes, because one is never sure the assumptions hold exactly.

Table 4.1.2   Exact and Approximate Calculations for the z-test: Sample Sizes for 90 and 99% Power, 5% One Tailed

δ	Δ	90% Power		99% Power	
		Exact	Approximate	Exact	Approximate
0.1	0.10	857	851	1578	1567
0.2	0.20	215	209	395	384
0.3	0.29	96	97	176	178
0.4	0.38	54	54	99	99
0.5	0.46	35	36	64	65
0.6	0.54	24	25	44	45
0.7	0.60	18	18	33	33
0.8	0.66	14	15	25	26
0.9	0.72	11	11	20	20
1.0	0.76	9	<10	16	17

4.2 Single-Sample t-test

In the z-test example above, we used the background information to establish the standard deviation in the population ($\sigma = 7$) for use in the test. The studies available for exploratory research, however, are done at a different time and a different place, and this information may not apply to the population now under study. If the "known" standard deviation were in error, the test we proposed to apply (the z-test) might not be valid. Consequently, we might hesitate to stake the validity of our final test result on what may be a shaky "knowledge" of the variance. Instead, we might propose to use a single-sample t-test in which we *estimate* the population standard deviation in the sample we obtain rather than using a value from a potentially different population.

We continue to assume that the responses are normally distributed with unknown mean μ but now with unknown variance σ^2, and we propose to reject $H_0 : \mu \le \mu_0$ (a one-tailed test) if

$$\sqrt{n}(\mu - \mu_0)/s \ge t_{n-1,\alpha},$$

where n is the sample size, μ is the sample mean, and s^2 is the sample variance. To use the master tables

$$\delta = (\mu - \mu_0)/\sigma, \tag{4.2.1}$$

$$\Delta = \delta/(\delta^2 + 1)^{1/2},$$

$$n = v + 1.$$

Again, one might use this δ (the same as in the single-sample z-test) as the effect size or Δ (now different from the single-sample z-test) or SRD—whichever of these seems more interpretable should be used—and its estimate and confidence interval reported as part of the results.

The critical value δ^* remains 0.5. However, the corresponding Δ is now different (4.2.1), because this is a different test. One needs a slightly larger sample size if one is to estimate σ as opposed to when one knows σ. The value of Δ corresponding to the critical values now is 0.45, not 0.46 as it would have been for a one-tailed 5% level z-test when the variance was known. This means, of course, that the necessary sample size will increase somewhat. From the master table, for a 5% one-tailed test with 90% power, the value of v now is 38, and since now $n = v + 1$, the necessary sample size is 39, not 35 as it would have been for the z-test. To protect the validity of the test, we are obliged to obtain four more participants—not a bad price to ensure validity.

Table 4.2.1 shows the approximate sample size for the z-test and for the t-test, for 5% level tests with 90% and 99% power for a range of δ values. Clearly, the necessary sample size is always greater for the t-test than for the z-test, but the small increase is usually well worthwhile to protect the validity of the test. In fact, in our years of experience, we cannot recall ever recommending using a one-sample z-test in preference to a one-sample t-test.

4.3 Two-Sample t-test

The two-sample t-test is probably the most commonly used statistical test. Suppose the total sample of n participants splits into two groups, with a proportion p coming from one group and a proportion q from the second group ($p + q = 1$). The scores in both groups are assumed to be normally distributed with the same variance, but the first group has mean μ_1 and the second group, mean μ_2. Here let us say that the null hypothesis is $H_0: \mu_1 \geq \mu_2$, a one-tailed test.

Table 4.2.1 σ^2 Known Versus σ^2 Unknown: Sample Sizes for Single-Sample z- and t-tests for 90 and 99% Power, 5% One Tailed

			90% Power		99% Power	
	Δ	Δ	n	N	N	n
δ	σ^2 Known	σ^2 Unkown	σ^2 Known	σ^2 Unkown	σ^2 Known	σ^2 Unkown
0.1	0.10	0.10	851	853	1567	1569
0.2	0.20	0.20	209	211	384	386
0.3	0.29	0.29	97	99	178	180
0.4	0.38	0.37	54	60	99	108
0.5	0.46	0.45	36	39	65	70
0.6	0.54	0.51	25	30	45	53
0.7	0.60	0.57	18	23	33	41
0.8	0.66	0.62	15	19	26	33
0.9	0.72	0.67	11	16	20	27
1.0	0.76	0.71	<10	14	17	23

With the two-sample t-test, we would propose to reject H_o when

$$(npq)^{1/2} (M_1 - M_2)/s \geq t_{n-2,\alpha},$$

where M_1 and M_2 are the two-sample means and s^2 is the pooled within-group variance. One can then use the master table with

$$\delta = (\mu_1 - \mu_2)/\sigma, \qquad (4.3)$$

$$\Delta = \delta/(\delta^2 + 1/pq)^{1/2},$$

$$N = v + 2.$$

The parameter δ has sometimes been called "Glass's effect size" or, more commonly, "Cohen's d" and has enjoyed extensive use in meta-analyses. In that context, researchers have been urged to publish either the values of Cohen's d for their own research projects or to publish the descriptive statistics (i.e., the means and standard deviations) necessary to the calculations of Cohen's d. Routine publication of such information would facilitate not only meta-analyses but also cost-effective planning of future research in related areas.

Note that the Δ defined in Equation (4.3) for the two-sample t-test is now not an effect size, since it incorporates p and q, which reflect the decision of the researchers and are not population parameters.

Generally, researchers tend to try to equalize the group size (set $p = q = 1/2$) since that would maximize the Δ for any fixed value of δ (and thus minimize the necessary sample size). However, there are many situations in which one group may require much more time, effort, and cost than the other group. By assigning a greater proportion of participants to the less expensive group (p > 1/2), one can afford to recruit a much larger sample size for the same cost but greater power. It should be emphasized that it is a valid research design choice to have imbalance in the sample sizes—we have occasionally met researchers who mistakenly view imbalance as a sign of an invalid design.

As seen in Table 4.3.1, the greater the imbalance (as either p or q nears zero), the smaller the Δ corresponding to the critical effect size and thus the larger the necessary sample size. To achieve maximal power from a fixed sample size, equalize the group sizes. However, what is also to be noticed in Table 4.3.1 is that the effect size changes very slowly as p moves between about .25 to .75. In short, there will be very little sacrifice in power for a slight to moderate imbalance between group sizes. Beyond those limits, the effect size plummets and the sample size rockets.

For a critical value of δ^* of 0.5, for example, moving from perfect balance ($p = q = 0.5$) to a 90–10 split (i.e., 90% in one group, 10% in the other), the critical effect size decreases from 0.24 to 0.15. Thus, for a 5% one-tailed test and 80% power, a 50–50 split requires 107 participants, a 70–30 split requires 127 participants (125 + 2), an 80–20 split requires 154 participants (152 + 2), and a 90–10 split, 274 participants (272 + 2). Epidemiological studies usually require very large sample sizes, frequently in the thousands. Such studies often compare groups with and without a certain disorder or disease that is relatively rare in the general population. The result is a gross imbalance in group sizes in a representative sample from a population, which necessitates a very large sample size for enough power to detect even quite large effects as well as to ensure credibility of the results. In other contexts, such as medical clinical trials or psychological experiments, sample sizes need be nowhere near as large, for the researchers can choose to balance the sample sizes.

In the earlier examples, using the single-sample z-test or t-test, we compared coffee drinkers with what would be expected from historical information. However, such information, from a study done in another time and locale, may not well represent what is true in the time or locale of the current research. Over the years since that study was done, men may have grown healthier (or less so) or more variable (or less so). If any of these changes have occurred, using either the single-sample z-test or the single-sample t-test may be invalid in the current study. Historical information must suffice to help plan the study, but unnecessarily risking an invalid test result by depending too strongly on that information for the final study result may not be a sound strategy.

Instead, we might propose to obtain a concurrent control group of non-coffee drinkers against which to compare our group of moderate-coffee drinkers. As above, we will take as our critical value of Cohen's d, $\delta^* = 0.5$. In this case, one might draw a large representative sample from the population and discard all but the non-coffee drinkers and the heavy coffee drinkers, a tactic that will usually lead to unequal sample sizes in the two groups. Alternatively one might simply recruit an equal number in the two extreme groups ensuring balance. In either case, the power calculations are those for the two-sample t-test above. There may be difference in the costs of recruitment in these situations, but the latter strategy would likely minimize the costs of follow-up.

4.4 An Exercise in Planning

Often researchers must choose between various designs, each of which ends with a t-test but with widely differing power. For example, suppose exploratory studies clearly indicate that heavy coffee drinking impairs health. As a result, we are now considering an intervention on heavy coffee drinkers to reduce health risk and want to demonstrate the effectiveness of that intervention.

Table 4.3.1 Two-Sample t-test: Critical Effect Sizes (Δ) for Balanced (p = q = .5) and Unbalanced (p ≠ q) Group Sizes

δ	p, q =				
	0.5	**0.6**	**0.7**	**0.8**	**0.9**
		0.4	**0.3**	**0.2**	**0.1**
0.1	0.05	0.05	0.05	0.04	0.03
0.2	0.10	0.10	0.09	0.08	0.06
0.3	0.15	0.15	0.14	0.12	0.09
0.4	0.20	0.19	0.18	0.16	0.12
0.5	0.24	0.24	0.22	0.20	0.15
0.6	0.29	0.28	0.27	0.23	0.18
0.7	0.33	0.32	0.31	0.27	0.21
0.8	0.37	0.36	0.34	0.30	0.23
0.9	0.41	0.40	0.38	0.34	0.26
1.0	0.45	0.44	0.42	0.37	0.29

OPTION 1: THE SINGLE-SAMPLE PRE-POST DESIGN

Heavy coffee drinkers are to be recruited (say those who report drinking more than six cups per day) who are between 20 and 40 years of age, and each will be treated and followed for five years. We propose to measure their age-adjusted CMI (CMI-A) at the baseline and then at the end of the five-year follow-up. A matched pair t-test is proposed to test whether the CMI-A is reduced with a 5% one-tailed test.

Now because we are using an age-adjusted score, the change in CMI-A over the five years under the null hypothesis should average 0. Thus our null hypothesis is $H_0: \mu_1 - \mu_2 \leq 0$.

We would use this information with

$$\delta = (\mu_2 - \mu_1) / \sigma[2(1-\rho)]^{1/2}$$
$$\Delta = \delta / (\delta^2 + 1)^{1/2},$$
$$n = \nu + 1,$$

where μ_2 is the mean CMI-A for coffee drinkers at the end of five years, μ_1 is the mean CMI-A for coffee drinkers at the entry to the study, and ρ is the correlation coefficient between the CMI-A at entry and that five years later, which we can estimate from the exploratory studies on which the age adjustment for CMI were based.

Let us stop here, because there are major problems with this design: *statistical regression to the mean and expectation effects.*

Statistical regression to the mean. When participants for an intervention study are selected because they are in the extremes of the distribution of some baseline variable (here more than six cups of coffee a day) and the baseline variable is not perfectly reliably measured (almost inevitably true), there is a statistical artifact generated: an apparent move of that variable measured in follow-up toward the center of the distribution even in absence of any actual change in what that variable measures (Campbell & Kenny, 1999). Thus here, even if the intervention did not change coffee drinking at all, we might expect to see an apparent decrease in coffee consumption whatever the treatment. The reason for this is simple. In selecting participants, because of the unreliability, there will be both false positive (overestimation of true coffee drinking level) and false negatives (underestimation). However, in the selection, false positives will be included and false negatives excluded. Upon follow-up, the false positives are likely to be measured closer to their true level (lower than their entry value), and if no one actually changes, that will create an overall *appearance* of decrease. Consequently, seeing a decrease in coffee drinking in a pre-post study among those selected because their initial coffee drinking was high (more than six cups a day), does not necessarily mean that coffee drinking actually did decrease—it may be an illusion. The more unreliable the measure used in selection and the more extreme the cut-point used, the stronger that illusion may be. Moreover, any variable (health status?) strongly associated with coffee drinking will be affected as well.

Expectation effects. Participants in a study, having signed informed consent forms that explain the intervention and its purpose, and the researchers conducting the study, who know that all participants are given the treatment, develop an expectation of improvement that can affect their measurement of improvement. Yogi Berra is quoted as saying "If I had not believed it, I would not have seen it!" and that pertains here. Thus one may see what appears to be an improvement when there is none—another illusion—because of the biases introduced into the measurement process by expectation effects.

The upshot is that even if one sees what appears to be an improvement in a one-sample study, how much of that improvement is an illusion because of these and other statistical artifacts and how much is real, cannot be ascertained.

As a result, a one-sample pre-post study is not a valid study design to show the effectiveness of any intervention.

Indeed, one of the most common errors in the research literature occurs when, following a randomized clinical trial comparing two treatments that could not demonstrate differential effectiveness, researchers do a one-sample pre-post comparison in the two treatment groups separately. With a reasonable sample size, they are often able to show a statistically significant "improvement" in both groups. The interpretation then is that both treatments were equally effective, whereas the truth may be that neither had any effect, but both were equally affected by statistical artifacts.

The bottom line is, we would not recommend using any single-sample test to show effectiveness of a treatment. The issue is validity, not power.

OPTION 2: TWO-SAMPLE ENDPOINT STUDY

The upshot of the above discussion is that to test the effectiveness of an intervention, we need a concurrent control group. Let us propose to sample participants as before (heavy coffee drinkers) but now randomly assign half to the intervention and half to a placebo treatment (one unlikely to change coffee-drinking behavior). We propose to compare the CMI-A at the end of the five-year follow-up between these two groups, using a one-tailed two-sample t-test at the 5% significance level. Both participants and any researchers involved in assessing outcomes will be "blinded" to which is the active treatment and which is the placebo to avoid biasing their assessments.

In this case, according to the master tables

$$\delta = (\mu_2 - \mu_1) / \sigma,$$
$$\Delta = \delta / (\delta^2 + 4)^{1/2}, \text{ (balanced design)}$$
$$n = \nu + 2.$$

Here μ_2 is the mean age-corrected CMI of those in the treatment group and μ_1 is the mean age-corrected CMI of those in the control group.

Now, with the randomized design, the two samples are random samples drawn from the same population. With random assignment and "blinding," the same statistical artifacts that affect one group will also affect the other. Differences found at follow-up between the two groups are then valid indications of effectiveness of the treatment and, with the randomized clinical trial methodology, would also support a causal effect of coffee drinking on health.

If the critical effect size remains $\delta^* = .5$, then the corresponding $\Delta = .24$. To have more than 80% power to detect any effect size greater than that, one finds $\nu = 105$, which, since we propose to have equal numbers in the two groups, means that $n = 107$ or 54 participants per treatment group. (We always round up any fractional participants!)

But why, some would ask, are we only focusing on comparing the endpoint measure when we know that some participants started in good health and others in very poor health? Would it not be better to examine the individual change scores, thus acknowledging the distance each individual participant has traveled during the treatment period?

OPTION 3: TWO-SAMPLE PRE-POST DESIGN

The sampling and design now remain the same, but for each participant the outcome measure is now the change in age-adjusted CMI from baseline to the five-year follow-up rather than the endpoint. Again, we propose to use a two-sample t-test and a one-tailed 5% test to compare the two groups on the pre-post change scores. Now

$$\delta = (\mu_2 - \mu_1)/\sigma[2(1-\rho)]^{1/2}, t$$
$$\Delta = \delta/(\delta^2 + 4)^{1/2},$$
$$n = \nu + 1,$$

where μ_2 is the mean change in CMI-A for those in the intervention group and μ_1 is the mean change in CMI-A among those in the control group. Here the population δs differ from those for the endpoint design because the variance of the change score is different from the variance of the endpoint score—how different determined by the correlation between the pre- and post-scores (ρ). All responses, both pre- and post-treatment, are assumed to have equal within-group variance (σ^2), and the correlation between pre- and post-treatment measures, ρ, is assumed to be the same in both treatment groups.

Which design would you prefer if the decision were to be based strictly on statistical validity and power? Which would be most cost-effective?

Table 4.4.1 shows the critical effect sizes when the correlation (ρ) between pre- and post-measures are 0.1, 0.5, and 0.9 and when Cohen's effect size (δ) is 0.1, 0.5, and 1.0.

The single-sample pre-post study always has the maximal effect size, which means the minimum necessary sample size. However, as we've pointed out, this design has questionable validity. We include this design here only to emphasize the fact that the first and foremost consideration must be to have a valid test. Only after validity is guaranteed is the question of power an issue.

A Type I error in statistical hypothesis testing is a false positive claim, meaning the study supports one's hypothesis when the null hypothesis is true. Statistical significance is the probability of a Type I error. A Type II error is a false negative result, being unable to support one's hypothesis when that hypothesis is true. Power is the probability of avoiding a Type II error. Some have proposed that a useful definition of a Type III error is asking the wrong research question in the first place. Occasionally a researcher will propose to use a questionably valid design and test because there is greater power, thus getting the right answer to the wrong question, which is not necessarily good science. That would be a Type III error. We would not propose to use a one-sample test to evaluate the effectiveness of an intervention.

That leaves the two-sample tests. With the two-sample designs, when $\rho = 0.5$, the endpoint and pre-post designs have equal critical effect size (see Table 4.4.1) and therefore require equal sample size. However, these designs may differ in cost, for the endpoint design requires only one measure per participant, whereas the pre-post design requires two, separated by the five years of follow-up. It is true that any additional measure takes up the time of participants and personnel and therefore increases effort and cost. In this case, when $\rho = 0.5$, any additional expenditure for the pre-post design is wasted, for there is no resulting increase in the effectiveness of the design.

However, it is often true that, even if the baseline measurement of the outcome is not used in testing hypotheses, it is obtained in order to well characterize the population to whom the results apply. In that case, when $\rho = .5$, it

Table 4.4.1   Critical Effect Sizes (Δ) for One-Sample Pre-Post, Two-Sample Endpoint, and Pre-Post Designs

		Single-Sample Pre-Post	Two-Sample Endpoint	Two-Sample Pre-Post
δ	ρ	Δ	Δ	Δ
0.1	0.1	0.07	0.05	0.04
0.1	0.5	0.10	0.05	0.05
0.1	0.9	0.22	0.05	0.11
0.5	0.1	0.35	0.24	0.18
0.5	0.5	0.45	0.24	0.24
0.5	0.9	0.75	0.24	0.49
1.0	0.1	0.60	0.45	0.35
1.0	0.5	0.71	0.45	0.45
1.0	0.9	0.91	0.45	0.75

doesn't matter whether you use the endpoint or the repeated measures design in terms of either power or cost.

When $\rho < 0.5$, the endpoint design has more power. When $\rho > 0.5$, the two-sample pre-post design does. When assessing a trait that is relatively stable over time and characteristic of the participant, using a change score will increase power. When assessing a state (or an unstable trait) or using an outcome measure with low reliability, endpoint designs are preferable.

It is important for researchers to realize that, as in this case, there is no universal answer to the question "Which design is better?" Which is a better design always depends on the nature of the specific research question as well as on the nature of the response in the population to be studied. Such matters are better understood by the researcher who is expert in that field and familiar with the research already done in that field than by any consultant statistician, no matter how expert in the field of statistics. This is particularly true when the feasibility and cost of the three designs must be simultaneously considered—as they invariably must be.

OPTION 4: TWO-SAMPLE DESIGN WITH REPEATED ENDPOINT MEASURES

It is quite common that, as in the comparison between the endpoint and pre-post designs, the choice between designs comes down to some issue related to some quality of the outcome measure. There, it was the correlation between the pre- and post-measures. However, another almost universal issue is the test-retest reliability of the outcome measure.

Any observed measure (here CMI-A) has some error of measurement, that is,

observed outcome (O) = true (T) + error (E),

where T is the mean of repeated independent measurements of O within a time span in which T is constant. Here we assume that the mean of E is zero and that E is independent of T. The reliability of a single measurement of O in a population is defined as

$$\text{reliability } (\rho_1) = \text{variance (true)/variance (observed)}$$
$$\rho_1 = \sigma^2_T / (\sigma^2_O) = \sigma^2_T/(\sigma^2_T + \sigma^2_E), \text{ and thus,}$$
$$\sigma^2_O = \sigma^2_T (1 - \rho_1)/\rho_1.$$

The less reliable the measure of O (ρ_1) in the population sampled, the more inflated the within-population variance of the measure in that population. Since the square root of that variance is in the denominator of the effect size δ, the less reliable the measure of O, the smaller the actual effect size. In fact, $\delta_O = \sqrt{\rho_1}\, \delta_T$, where δ_O is the population effect size for the observed measures and

δ_T is the population effect size for the true values of those measures. Thus, if the true population effect size were, say, .8, and if the reliability coefficient were .8 (a very reliable measure by most standards), the population effect size based on observed values would be .72, an attenuation. If ρ_1 were .6, the attenuated effect size would be .62; if ρ_1 were .4, the attenuated effect size would be .51. In short, if one were to power a study to detect any true effect size above whatever one set as the critical effect size δ^*, but then proceeded to use a relatively unreliable measure of the outcome, that study might well end underpowered. Worse yet, the sample estimate of the effect size would also be of the attenuated population effect size, raising questions as to how important even a statistically significant result might be.

The message is clear. It is vitally important that all measures used in analysis be very reliably measured. One of the issues that might well be addressed in any pilot study is the test-retest reliability of the outcome measures in the population sampled and in the hands of those who will be assessing outcome in the study. Training might be provided initially to assure that all assessors are reliable, and monitoring during the study might be done to prevent "drift" in measurements over the duration of the study. Even then, there are many characteristics of interest and importance where the very best of available measures have reliability, say, in the .4 to .6 region.

If so, one might design the study to remove some of the effect of unreliability. Now as before, we propose to sample n participants from the population, randomly assign half to the intervention and half to the control group, and then to assess the CMI-A m times ($m > 1$) at the end of follow-up, each assessment independent of the others, and to use the average of those m CMI-As for each participant as the outcome measure in a two-sample endpoint design.

It has long been known that averaging multiple independent measures of the same outcome increases reliability. In fact, under the assumption that E is independent of T, the reliability of the average of m measures per participant, ρ_m, is given by the Spearman-Brown projection formula (Brown, 1910; Spearman, 1910):

$$\rho_m = m\rho_1 / [(m - 1)\rho_1 + 1].$$

Then one can "step up" the reliability of any measure that has non-zero reliability to any level one chooses (theoretically), say ρ^*, simply by taking m participants where

$$m = \rho^*(1 - \rho_1)/[(1 - \rho^*)\rho_1].$$

The practical problem, of course, is that it is difficult to have multiple independent measures, but often $m = 3$ will do.

The mathematics here may be unfamiliar, but the principle should be familiar. Think of how often lab results are done in triplicate and the average used as the basis of clinical decisions. Think of the fact that judging athletic contests require multiple independent judges, where the average determines the contest outcome. The principle is intuitive as well as mathematical.

If we used the average of m independent measures at the end of follow-up instead of one, the effect size that would be $\delta_O = \sqrt{\rho_1}\,\delta_T$ with one measure, would then be $\delta_{Om} = \sqrt{\rho_m}\,\delta_T$, with the average of m measures, considerably larger. A larger effect size means that fewer participants are needed to have adequate power, reducing the duration and cost of the study. Moreover, if we used the average of m independent measures at baseline as well as at end of follow-up, that would stabilize those measures, making it more likely that the pre- and post-measures are highly correlated. Then, using a two-sample pre-post design would gain power both from increased reliability and from use of the change scores.

This discussion of reliability and its impact on effect sizes and thus on the answer to *How Many Subjects?* is not based on an assumption of normal distributions (although use of the t-tests is). However, there are two crucial assumptions in this discussion: that the error of measurement does not depend on the true value and that the multiple assessments for each individual participant are independent. Frequently, the error of measurement is greater for some ranges of the true value than for others, and often it is near impossible to guarantee the independence of multiple assessments per participant. Yet, in such cases, the principles continue to hold. Unreliability attenuates effect sizes. The greater the unreliability, the larger the sample size must be to compensate for the attenuation of effect sizes. One can step up reliability by taking linear combinations (e.g., averages) of multiple assessments and thus increase the effect size and decrease the sample size necessary for adequate power. What does not necessarily hold are the indications of how much attenuation in effect size there will be and how much improvement there would be by stepping up the reliability.

OPTION 5: TWO-SAMPLE DESIGN, SLOPE AS THE OUTCOME MEASURE

Let us consider one more, very attractive, possibility. Suppose sampling, randomization, blinding, baseline, and end of follow-up measures are taken as before (the measures as reliable as we can manage by careful selection, use of multiple assessments, etc.). However, now in addition to the measure at baseline (time $t_1 = 0$) and at end of follow-up (time $t_T = 1$), we propose to assess outcome measures at $T - 2$ intermediate time-points (at $t_2, t_3, \ldots t_{T-1}$) and to use the slope of outcome on time as the outcome measure. Where $T = 2$, there are no intermediate time points, and this is simply equivalent to the pre-post design discussed above.

Some will argue that the individual slope of outcome on time over the course of treatment is a better indication of treatment response than either the endpoint or the pre-post change. Putting as much dependence on the accuracy of the endpoint in both these designs means that a mismeasure at that one time-point can seriously misrepresent that participant's response. Using a measure of directional trend over time seems a safer choice.

Peto (1981) long ago made the observation that, at any time during a horse race, the position of a horse on the track (endpoint), the distance traveled from the opening gate (change score), and the horse's rate of speed (slope) will be perfectly correlated. For each individual participant

endpoint = baseline + average rate of change × duration of follow-up,

or

change = endpoint − baseline = average rate of change × duration of follow-up.

In a randomized clinical trial, as here, the mean baseline is the same for both groups, as is the duration of follow-up. Thus, at the population level, the mean difference in endpoints between the two groups is exactly equivalent to the mean difference in change, and both are directly proportional to the mean difference in average rate of change, that is, slope. In a randomized clinical trial, the horseracing effect suggests that an endpoint score, a change score, and a slope are all valid measures of essentially the same response. They do, however, differ in their reliability. All we need then argue about is whether the estimate of that slope is to be estimated from only pre- and post-measures or whether we will add intermediate time points for measurement, and, if so, how many and how spaced.

On the other hand, some criticize the notion of using a slope, claiming that this approach is appropriate only if the trajectory of outcome from baseline to end of follow-up for each participant is linear, and one can seldom guarantee a linear trajectory for all participants. However, as illustrated by Kraemer and Thiemann (1989), the slope estimate for an individual from a standard linear regression analysis can be written as

$$\text{slope} = \Sigma w_{jk}\, (O_j - O_k)/(t_j - t_k),$$

where the sum is taken over all pairs of time points, w_{jk} is a weight that depends only on the time points fixed by the researchers, and $(O_j - O_k)/(t_j - t_k)$ is the slope taken between two fixed time points. Thus, whatever the shape of the trajectory, linear or not, the estimate of slope from a linear regression represents the average slope over all the pairs of time points.

It is true that one might rescale the values of t_j to induce a greater linearity of the response trajectory. For example, in RCTs, the response trajectory more often has a fishhook shape with more rapid response earlier than later in the follow-up period than it does a straight line shape. Then, instead of coding the time point t_j as the number of days from baseline, one might code it as the t_j = Logarithm(number of days + 1). Then the response trajectory graphed as a function of t_j is often much closer to linear. To do this reduces the error variance somewhat and increases power. Like repeated measures of the same outcome at endpoint or baseline, using repeated measures over time to estimate a slope results in a linear combination of observed values, and this will tend to cancel some of the effects of unreliability. How much such cancellation takes place depends on the number and timing of the individual measures, on the spacing of the time points, and on the independence of errors of measurement over the time points. Generally, however, having several intermediate time points and basing the analysis (perhaps using hierarchical linear models) on comparing slopes in the two groups will yield much greater power than will the endpoint design or the pre-post design.

There is also a more subtle advantage to using a slope as an outcome measure. Use of the t-tests is based on the assumption of normally distributed observations in both groups, with equal variances. It is generally true that, whatever the distribution of a single observation in the two populations, the distribution of a linear combination of many single observations per participant is more likely to have at least an approximately normal distribution. In many cases, where the use of a t-test for a single endpoint measure or a change score based on single measurements pre- and post-treatment is of questionable validity because the measure is on a 2-, 3-, 4- . . . point scale rather than a continuum or is a measure on a continuum with a skew or long-tailed distribution, the same t-test will be valid for a linear combination of enough such measures for each individual. The remaining concern for validity would be that of equal variances in the two groups. However, it is known that the t-test is quite robust to unequal variances provided the design is balanced ($p = q = .5$), yet another argument for preferring balanced designs (costs being equal).

Moreover, in considering power issues in designing a study, we tend to ignore the possibility of missing data problems. Yet in reality, missing data in studies of human participants are almost inevitable. Since valid analysis of a randomized clinical trial requires analysis "by intention to treat," some of the several methods of dealing appropriately with missing data in the analysis must be used. Every such method does better, the more information one has on each participant. Thus if a participant drops out anytime during the study, one is missing the crucial endpoint as well as the change score, and there is no information on that participant's response to treatment prior to dropout. However, including measurements of outcome at several intermediate time points early in the follow-up adds information on that participant's response trajectory and would provide partial information on treatment response and facilitate successful use of imputation methods.

In short, use of the slope of response on time over the follow-up period offers many advantages in planning a study.

4.5 Controversial Issues

Remember that Cohen's d in a two-sample design is closely related to AUC = Probability(X > Y) + .5Probability(X = Y). In effect, using Cohen's d as the effect size in a two-sample design means that we are essentially comparing the response (however measured) of each participant against each participant in the other treatment group. The answer one gets indicates whether in the preponderance of such pairwise comparisons, T1 is preferred to T2 or vice versa.

Yet, what every participant and clinician wants to know is not how much better off **I** would be with T1 rather than all those in the T2, many very different from me, but how much better off **I** would be compared with others **like me.** We don't want to compare **MY** response to all participants given the other treatment but only to those participants similar to **ME** at baseline. If you accept this argument, then in choosing to use a two-sample design we may be committing a Type III error, asking the wrong question.

At least three solutions have been proposed to deal with the issue: a crossover design, randomized matched pair design, and a regression analysis. Let us discuss the first two approaches here and return to this problem later to discuss the regression analysis approach. All of these approaches may be controversial.

OPTION 6: A CROSSOVER DESIGN

The ideal, of course, is to compare each participant's response to T1 to his or her own response to T2, often described as "using the participant as his or her own control." What is often proposed to do this is a crossover design, in which a sample of n participants is drawn from the population of interest, half are assigned to T1 and half to T2, each treated and evaluated as in a simple two-sample design. Then a "wash-out" period occurs, during which all the effects of that first treatment are allowed to disappear. Then those assigned initially to T1 are given T2 ("crossed over") and those assigned initially to T2 are given T1 and evaluation is done exactly as in the first period.

If we assume that complete washout has occurred, the simplest analysis is to compute the T1 versus T2 difference for each participant. If there are time effects, these will cancel out. Then a matched pairs t-test can be used with

$$\delta = (\mu_1 - \mu_2)/[\sigma(2(1 - \rho)^{1/2}],$$

$$\Delta = \delta/(\delta^2 + 1)^{1/2},$$

$$v = n - 1.$$

The problem here lies in the fact that the validity of the test depends on the assumption that after the wash-out period, every participant returns to virgin status, that is, exactly the same participant he or she was prior to the first period. This is seldom true. There are almost inevitably carry-over effects from the first treatment to the second. If one treatment involved education of some sort, the effects of that treatment will never be washed out. The metabolites of a drug treatment may last far longer than the half-life of the drug. If one treatment is very effective, those participants having that treatment first may be unwilling to give it up and will tend to drop out. If one treatment has serious side effects, that might also prompt dropout. If one treatment is very effective, its effect may long outlast the wash out period, and the participant will be very different at the beginning of the second treatment from what he or she was at the first.

If one does a crossover design, it is important that there be a check for carry-over effects before any results are reported (a more complicated analysis [Brown, 1980]). However, the sample size necessary for adequate power to detect even important carry-over effects can be much larger than that needed to do a simple two-sample design. Moreover, the fallback analysis, if carry-over effects are detected, is to discard the second period entirely and to do a simple two-sample test on responses in the first period of the crossover design. However, if the design was powered using both periods, discarding the second period will frequently result in an underpowered study if only the first period can be used. In summary, many statisticians and researchers may disagree, but we would always recommend against doing a crossover design, not from considerations of power but of considerations of validity.

OPTION 7: A RANDOMIZED MATCHED-PAIR DESIGN

Since we can't "use each participant as his or her own control," a phrase used to cover the situation addressed in the crossover design, we might instead "control for" a baseline variable B in a matched-pairs design. Now we will sample n pairs of participants, each pair matched on specific baseline values, and randomly assign one of each pair to T1, the other to T2. Again assessment of outcome is "blinded" to treatment and to pairings, and outcome is measured as best one can (endpoint? change? slope?). We will continue to assume that the distribution of outcomes in the two groups is normal with equal variances and propose to use a matched-pairs t-test, that is, a single-sample t-test on the paired differences.

Now we meet other problems. Figure 4.5.1 illustrates three situations with very different implications. In each case, a baseline variable (B) is shown on the horizontal axis, and the outcome measure (O) on the vertical axis, with the expected outcomes for participants in the two treatment groups (T1 and T2) shown (to ease the discussion) as two straight lines.

A baseline variable (B) is *irrelevant to treatment response in an RCT* if it is predictive of the mean response in neither of the two treatment groups (Figure 4.5.1 (a)). With a linear response pattern, this would mean two flat lines relating O to B in the two treatment groups. A baseline variable (B) is a nonspecific predictor of treatment response in an RCT if it is predictive of response to both T1 and T2, but the treatment effect comparing T1 versus T2 between two participants with the same B is the same regardless of what B is (e.g., Figure 4.5.1 (b)). With a linear response pattern, this would mean two non-flat parallel lines in the two treatment groups. Finally B is a *moderator of treatment response in an RCT*, if the treatment effect comparing T1 versus T2 between two participants with the same B differs depending on what the value of B is (e.g, Figure 4.5.1 (c)). With a linear response pattern, this would mean two non-parallel lines in the two treatment groups.

Then to use the master tables,

$$\delta = (\mu_1 - \mu_2)/\sigma(2(1 - \rho))^{1/2},$$

$$\Delta = \delta/(\delta^2 + 1)^{1/2},$$

$$v = n - 1.$$

Here $\mu_1 - \mu_2$ is the mean paired difference, σ^2 the variance of responses in the two treatment groups, assumed to be the same, ρ the correlation between the paired outcomes, and n is the number of pairs to be sampled, that is, *2n* participants to be followed.

With this matched pairs design, we are now comparing each participant only against another participant with the same baseline B, and thus we've changed the research question from that addressed in a one-sample design. What have we changed it to?

To illustrate the problems with this proposal, let us assume that each individual outcome measure is given by

$$O = \beta_0 + \beta_1 I + \beta_2 B + \beta_3 IB + E.$$

Here I represents choice of treatment, set equal to +1/2 if the T1 is assigned and −1/2 if T2 is assigned. B is the baseline variable, coded to have a mean of zero and a variance of one in the population sampled. Note that with randomization the population distribution of B is the same in both T1 and T2. E is the error and is assumed to have mean 0 and to be independent of I and B, with error

Figure 4.5.1   Potential moderation: (a) *B* is irrelevant to treatment outcome, (b) *B* is a nonspecific predictor of treatment outcome, and (c) *B* is a moderator of treatment outcome

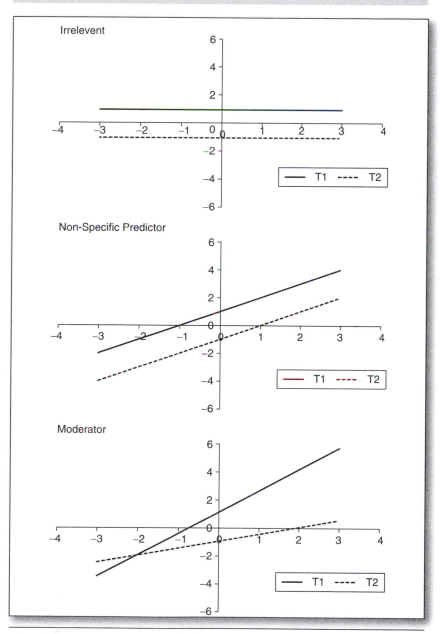

A baseline variable defines the horizontal axis. The outcome measures the vertical axis. The mean response for participants with each baseline value in the T1 and T2 groups are represented as two straight lines.

variance σ^2_E. In this approach, β_1 is often called the "treatment effect," and this is interpreted as the effect of treatment for every subject compared to others with the same B. Then β_2, is the "main effect of B" on O, and β_3, is the "interactive effect of treatment and B." This is a classical linear model to describe the situation shown in Figure 4.5.1. If B is irrelevant to treatment outcome, then $\beta_2 = \beta_3 = 0$. If B is a nonspecific predictor of treatment outcome, then $\beta_2 \neq 0$ and $\beta_3 = 0$. If B is a moderator of treatment outcome, then $\beta_3 \neq 0$.

Now the expected mean difference between treatment group responses (coded as we have) in the two-group design is β_1, and in the matched pairs test is β_1, but for a subpopulation matched on a specific M, it is $\beta_1 + \beta_3 M$, which equals β_1 only when B is not a moderator of treatment response. If B is a moderator of treatment response, there is no one answer to the question "How good is this treatment for me compared to others like me (in B)? The answer differs depending on what B is. It doesn't matter which approach is taken—the answer one obtains is that for the typical participant$(M = 0)$, not for any participant.

Then (making normality and equal variance assumptions), if a two-sample test were used,

$$\delta = \beta_1/(\beta_2^2 + .25\beta_3^2 + \sigma^2_E)^{1/2}$$

$$\Delta = \delta/(\delta^2 + 4)^{1/2} \text{ (balanced design)},$$

$$v = n - 2 \ (n \text{ the number of participants)}.$$

If a matched-pairs test were used,

$$\delta = \beta_1/(\beta_3^2 + 2\sigma^2_E)^{1/2},$$

$$\Delta = \delta/(\delta^2 + 1)^{1/2}$$

$$v = n - 1 \ (n \text{ the number of pairs}).$$

Which of these two tests is more powerful to test the null hypothesis they both test depends on the reliability of the measure used (σ^2_E) and then on the relative magnitudes of the effect of B on O and the interactive effect of treatment by B (β_2 and β_3). The bottom line is that one needs to have a great deal of information on which baseline measures (B) affect treatment outcome in the two groups and exactly how they do so, to make the right decision as to how best to design the study. Moreover, one can interpret what results in either case as the treatment effect on all participants regardless of the B value, only if it is known that B is NOT a moderator of treatment response. Otherwise, the treatment effect should only be interpreted as the treatment effect on the typical participant with $B = 0$.

There are two messages here: One should not consider "controlling for" any baseline variable that has not already been shown in previous studies to be related to outcome in one or another of the treatment groups, and how one might "control" may be different. The earliest studies comparing two treatments should be simple two-sample designs, "controlling for" no baseline variables. However, when that study is completed, exploratory analyses should be done, using the data from that study, to determine which baseline variables are likely to be irrelevant to treatment outcome and which variables are either nonspecific predictors or moderators of treatment response. These exploratory studies then set up the rationale and justification for future studies that would take baseline characteristics into account, but do so appropriately.

Currently, many researchers argue that all sorts of baseline variables should be "controlled for": age, sex, education level, race, ethnicity, and so forth. This is done just in case any of these are associated with outcome. Most baseline variables are irrelevant to treatment outcome. Some are nonspecific predictors, and fewer are moderators, but the correct approach to deal with each such baseline variable differs depending on how it related to outcome. Often statistical methods are used that assume that these baseline variables are not moderators, perhaps without realizing that including any that are either irrelevant to treatment outcome or nonspecific predictors, always decreases power and increases the cost and difficulty of the study for no gain, but frequently may compromise validity as well.

4.6 Balanced Analysis of Variance (ANOVA)

The matched-pair t-test and the two-sample t-test are both designed to compare two means. There are many situations, however, when there are more than two means of interest. In the analysis of variance (ANOVA) approach, factors, each measured at several levels, define a number of cells, the means of which are compared in the analysis.

For example, a researcher may decide to simultaneously investigate the effects of drinking regular coffee (R), drinking only decaffeinated coffee (D), and abstinence from drinking coffee at all (A) by sampling an equal number of participants from each of these groups (balanced design) and measuring their CMI-As. There are now three possible paired group comparisons (R versus D), (R versus A), and (D versus A) that might be done in separate studies, but here we propose to have all three groups in one study. (We might equally well consider randomization to three interventions: a placebo, a behavioral intervention, and a medical intervention on heavy coffee drinkers).

If we assume that the outcomes measures within each group are normally distributed with equal variances, we might propose to use a one-way analysis of variance (ANOVA) to test the null hypothesis that $\mu_1 = \mu_2 = \mu_3 = \ldots \mu_G$ against the alternative that some groups differ from each other (the omnibus test).

Cohen, in his book on power (1988), and others give tables to compute power for this test and propose an effect size that compares the variance among the G population means with the within-group variance, which he calls f (Chapter 8). The mathematical logic of doing this is impeccable, and we would agree with the proposal here to use the one-way ANOVA, but we would choose another tactic for planning the study. We have found that when we use Cohen's approach, we may find a statistically significant result (supporting the hypothesis that the G population means differ), but the researchers then ask the obvious question: Which group differs significantly from which other? There are several statistical approaches to address such a question, but if the study is powered using Cohen's approach, there is often not enough power to answer the pairwise comparison problem well.

Consequently, we recommend that the researcher consider the pairwise mean comparisons of specific interest, one at a time, and use the two-sample method to compute the necessary sample size required per paired group. The total sample size that results will be larger than the total sample size for the omnibus test (testing the equality of all the means) as determined by Cohen's approach, but results in less frustration at the end of the study. If, for example, the critical effect size $\delta^* = .5$, then Δ for each pair of interventions is .24, and the total sample size for each pair of interventions is 146 or 73 per group, for a total of 219 participants in a three group study, 292 in a four group study.

4.7 Discussion

There are a number of messages here that generalize beyond t-tests and one-way ANOVA:

- Validity is always the first consideration. Only when validity is secured, does the issue of power become salient.
- A Type I error is controlled in setting the significance level. A Type II error is the topic of this discussion, related to designing a study with adequate power. It is important also to be aware of Type III error, which is asking or answering the wrong question. When this happens, the answer is often misinterpreted and misleads.
- The answer to the question *How Many Subjects?* is always an approximation. This is true even when the calculations are exact, not approximations as in the use of the master tables, because it is never assured that all the assumptions that underlie exact calculations hold.
- Any assumptions that can be avoided should be avoided. In these tests. we assume normal distributions and equal variances, which may be justified. However, assuming that one "knows" the variances or "knows" what the mean of a control population might be or other such assumptions should be avoided. This is an issue related to validity.

- There are arguments for balanced designs (here equal sample sizes in all groups), but there are situations where slightly unbalanced designs will result in more power at less cost.
- Above all, it is important to understand the importance of reliability of measures used in any analysis. Unreliability is the "noise" that covers up the "signals" one hopes to detect. We cannot overemphasize the importance of choosing the most reliability measures, of efforts (like training and monitoring) to maintain reliability over the course of the study, and of considering designs that compensate for the effects of unreliability on power.
- One should not consider "controlling for" any baseline variable that has not already been shown in previous studies to be related to outcome in one or another of the treatment groups, for how one might "control" may be different depending on whether that baseline variable is a nonspecific predictor or a moderator. If it is irrelevant, then it should not be controlled, for that only decreases power.
- It is important to understand that some mathematical results are intuitively obvious, like the impact of using a mean of repeated measures on reliability. Others are counter-intuitive, like the impact of using a matched-pairs design to estimate the effect of treatment on individual participants. In power considerations, mathematics always trumps intuition where these differ.
- Finally, it needs to be recognized that designing a valid, powerful, and cost-effective study to address any research question is a challenging creative exercise. It requires broad knowledge in the field of that research question and a sensitivity to all the problems that might occur and impair either the validity, the power, or the cost of the research study.

REFERENCES

Brown, W. (1910). Some experimental results in the correlation of mental abilities. *British Journal of Psychology, 3*, 296–322.

Brown, B. W., Jr. (1980). The crossover experiment for clinical trials. *Biometrics, 36*, 69–79.

Campbell, D. T., & Kenny, D. A. (1999). *A primer on regression artifacts*. New York: Guilford Press.

Cohen, J. (1988). *Statistical power analysis for the behavioral sciences*. Hillsdale, NJ: Lawrence Erlbaum.

Gordon, C., Emerson, A. R., & Simpson, J. (1959). The Cornell Medical Index Questionaire as a measure of health in socio-medical research. *Journal of Gerontology, 14*, 305–308.

Kraemer, H. C., & Thiemann, S. A. (1989). A strategy to use "soft" data effectively in randomized clinical trials. *Journal of Consulting and Clinical Psychology, 57*, 148–154.

Peto, R. (1981). The horse-racing effect. *Lancet, 318*(8244), 467–468.

Spearman, C. (1910). Correlation calculated from faulty data. *British Journal of Psychology, 3*, 271–295.

5

Correlation Coefficients

I n the last chapter, we considered tests of the equality of means. Frequently, however, research questions concern the *association* of variables rather than simply comparisons of means in one or more groups. For instance, rather than testing whether mean health status is higher among heavy coffee drinkers versus abstainers, we could ask a more general question: As coffee consumption increases, does health status decrease? Or vice versa? Formulating the question would carry the advantage that arbitrary cut points (heavy: over six cups a day; moderate: three to five cups a day; etc.) will not affect the conclusion. The most commonly used effect size to describe such an association is the Pearson product-moment correlation coefficient: ρ_P. While the two-sample t-test is arguably the most common test procedure in medical research, testing the Pearson correlation is undoubtedly the most common test in behavioral research.

Moreover, the last chapter discussed the crucial importance of reliability of measures to issues of power. Reliability is usually measured by a correlation coefficient, specifically the intraclass correlation coefficient: ρ_I. Since unreliability attenuates effect sizes and power for all statistical tests, determination of reliability via a correlation coefficient is fundamental to all statistical research designs. Let us start there.

5.1 Intraclass Correlation Coefficient

To assess the reliability of a measure, we draw a sample of n participants from the population of interest. (Reliability of a measure does change from one population to another!) For each participant, we obtain two independent measures taken in a time period in which the true value for the individual is unlikely to change.

If the interest is measurement of a characteristic at *one* time point in the view of *one* rater, this would mean *intra-rater* reliability, and one would have to have the same rater measure exactly the same response twice, each measurement "blinded" to the other to ensure independence. This is feasible only in special circumstances. For example, if a tissue sample is taken from each participant and the slides with that tissue sample are presented in random order with labels that carry no information to the rater, then six or 12 months later, the same set of n slides would be presented in a different random order with different labeling to the same rater, then the correlation between the two ratings per individual would be an intra-rater reliability. For most measures (those based on self-report, interview, or examination) it is difficult, if not impossible, to "blind" the rater to his or her own previous rating. Seldom is the reliability of a measure in the hands of one particular rater of interest.

If what is of interest is a measure of a characteristic at one time point by *some* rater, this would mean *inter-rater* reliability. For example, if the participant performs a certain task and two raters, randomly selected from a pool of raters, are asked to rate performance on that task, each without communication with the other, this would be inter-rater reliability. This type of reliability is often reported. However, the only error of measurement here considered is that due to raters, while a major source of unreliability is often the minute-to-minute, hour-to-hour, or day-to-day random fluctuations within an individual, even while the construct of interest (e.g., health status) remains unchanged.

Finally, if what is of interest is a measure of a characteristic in some span of time (a day, a week) we would assess *test-retest* reliability. Having the individual perform a certain task on two occasions several days apart, each rated by a different rater, each blinded to the other, picks up both error because of the rater and error because of random fluctuations. In most biobehavioral research, test-retest reliability is what most affects power of tests and precision of effect size estimates.

For instance, we might question how reliable a CMI-A is to characterize the individuals in the population of interest. If what one obtains in a self-report today poorly predicts what one would get tomorrow or on the next day, a period in which actual health status is unlikely to change, one might be justifiably wary of using this self-report.

Whichever type of reliability is of interest, the two ratings per individual should be randomly assigned to be the first ($X1$) and second ($X2$) positions for each individual. If there are time effects between the first and second rater or if the less-experienced rater is usually the first one or any other such consistent bias occurs between the two ratings, such bias is part of the error. Random assignment to the first and second position for each individual guarantees that it will be so assessed. This also guarantees that the population means and the population variances of the two ratings ($X1$ and $X2$) are the same.

The effect size here is ρ_1, the intraclass correlation coefficient. Since there are several different sample intraclass correlation coefficients, we need to specify that the one we deal with here is

$$r_1 = \Sigma(X1 - M1)(X2 - M2)/[.5(n-1)(s_1^2 + s_2^2)]^{1/2},$$

where $M1$ and $M2$ are the sample means of the ratings in the first and second positions, and s_1^2 and s_2^2 are the sample variances of the first and second ratings. Here, $M1$ and $M2$ are two estimates of the common population mean and s_1^2 and s_2^2 two estimates of the common population variance of the two ratings.

Suppose that $X1$ and $X2$ have a bivariate normal distribution. What this means is that

- $X1$ and $X2$ each have a normal distribution in the population of interest (normality assumptions for each);
- the means of $X2$ for fixed values of $X1$ are a linear function of $X1$, and the means of $X1$ for fixed values of $X2$ are a linear function of $X2$ (linearity assumption); and
- the variances of $X2$ for fixed values of $X1$ do not depend on $X1$ and vice versa (homoscedasticity or equal variance assumption).

In practice, this means that if one took a sample of n participants and created a scatter-diagram of X2 versus X1 across all participants, one would see a band of points following a straight line (linearity), and the width of that band, both horizontally and vertically, would be fairly uniform (homoscedasticity) across that line. Generally, correlation coefficients tend to be reasonably robust to deviations from the normality assumption but can be sensitive to serious deviations from the linearity and homoscedasticity assumptions.

In this case, we wish to demonstrate that the two scores correlate well, so our null hypothesis is not one of *no* correlation ($H_0 : \rho_0 = 0$) but rather one of some minimal association, say $H_0: \rho_1 \leq .5$, a one-tailed test. How many subjects are required to reject H_0 at the 5% level of significance with 90% power?

In this case, in the master table

$$\Delta = (\rho - \rho_0)/(1 - \rho\rho_0),$$

$$n = v + 1,$$

where ρ is the population correlation and ρ_0 is the value specified in the null hypothesis, here .5.

Suppose we felt that a correlation coefficient of 0.8 between physician interview and self-report CMI scores would be considered the critical value, because in the past literature, a value $\rho_1{}^* = .8$ and above have found wide acceptance and underlay successful studies. Then the associated Δ is

$$\Delta = (0.8 - 0.5)/[1 - (0.8)\ (0.5)] = 0.5.$$

For a one-tailed 5% test with 90% power, v is 30. Since $n = v + 1$, approximately 31 subjects are required for 90% power.

5.2 Product-Moment Correlation Coefficient

As always, the validity of a test depends on whether the data meet the assumptions of that test. While the intraclass correlation coefficient is based on the assumption that the two scores ($X1$ and $X2$, two measures of the same construct) come from a bivariate normal distribution, the Pearson product-moment correlation also assumes a bivariate normal distribution but between two *different* variables (now X and Y) and makes no assumption about equality of variance. In this case,

$$\Delta = (\rho - \rho_0)/(1 - \rho\rho_0),$$

$$n = v + 2.$$

Suppose we wanted to know how well a CMI-A based on self-report correlated with a full physician examination and interview resulting in a score between 0 (dead) and 100 (perfect health). This might be considered a test of the convergent validity of the CMI-A as a measure of health. We sample n participants from the population of interest (Correlation coefficients also change from one population to another!) and measure both variables X and Y on each participant, each measurement preferably "blinded" to the other.

"Blinding" here is optional but does affect the interpretation of conclusions. If the full physician examination is done first and that score is revealed to the participant before he or she fills out the CMI questionnaire, the participant may report quite differently from what he or she might have without seeing the physician's opinion (and vice versa). That would generally inflate the correlation coefficient and might mislead researchers as to how valid a CMI-A really is.

The CMI-A and the score may both have normal distributions, but since they are measured on different scales, there can be no expectation that the two means or variances are the same. To test the null hypothesis that the correlation between them (ρ) is less than .5, where the critical value was $\rho^* = .8$, we would find that for 90% power using a one-tailed 5% test:

$$\Delta = (0.8 - 0.5)/[1 - (0.8)\,(0.5)] = 0.5$$

$$n = v + 2 = 30 + 2 = 32.$$

The product-moment correlation can also be used when the two scores are measured on completely different scales, as long as the essential assumptions are satisfied. We might, for instance, decide to correlate average daily coffee consumption, measured in number of cups of coffee per day, with the CMI-A score. In this case, our null hypothesis is no association. The hypothesis test is now a two-tailed 5% test, since either direction is possible. We use the correlation coefficient considered important, say $\rho^* = 0.4$, as the critical effect size in our power calculations. Here, for 80% power

$$\Delta = (0.4 - 0)/1 - (0.4)\,(0) = 0.4,$$

$$n = v + 2 = 45 + 2 = 47.$$

Let us pause here to consider the problem of dichotomization or stratification in research studies. Earlier, we stratified the population, into ordinal categories of those who did not drink coffee (A), those who were low coffee drinkers (L: one to two cups a day), those who were moderate coffee drinkers (M: three to five cups a day), and those who were heavy coffee drinkers (H: six or more cups a day). We could regard these as four groups and use group comparison methods discussed earlier. Here we are considering instead simply using the actual number of cups per day as X and the CMI-A as Y and are testing their correlation. Which is preferred?

First of all, the cut points are arbitrary, and changing the cut points could change the conclusions drawn in comparing these groups on CMI-A. That would suggest that using the correlation approach might be better, since it does not depend on arbitrary cut points. Moreover, if the association between X and Y is linear or at least strictly monotonic (i.e., every additional cup per day adds to the health risk), use of the correlation coefficient will generate greater power to detect the association. However, if there is any possibility that good health is associated with moderate coffee drinking (however defined) and poor health with both extremes of coffee drinking, a non-monotonic association between coffee drinking and health status, the product-moment correlation coefficient will mislead. In that case, the product-moment correlation coefficient may even be zero, when there is a strong U-shaped association between X and Y. Here, what is observed in exploratory analyses must guide which approach to take.

The formula for the product-moment correlation coefficient is often applied to a pair of variables, X and Y, when the assumptions of bivariate normality do not hold. In that case, the correlation coefficient may still be meaningful, but the distribution theory of the product-moment correlation coefficient will not hold, and specifically, the master tables do not apply in considerations of power. To warn users that applying the formula to such data is a problem distinct from that addressed by ρ_p, the name of the coefficient is usually changed. Thus if X and Y were both binary measures (gender, success/failure on a task), the parameter estimated by r_p is called the "phi coefficient." If X is binary (gender) and Y has a normal distribution within both X groups with equal variances (thus satisfying t-test assumptions), it is called the *point biserial correlation coefficient.* If X has ordered categories (e.g., none, low, medium, heavy coffee drinking) and Y is normally distributed within each X group with equal variances (thus satisfying ANOVA assumptions), then it is called the *point multiserial correlation coefficient.* If X and Y are each rank ordered with ties assigned the average rank for which they are tied, r_p is called the *Spearman rank correlation coefficient.* Let us first consider the special case of rank correlation coefficients.

5.3 Rank Correlation Coefficients

Until now, the tests we have discussed to assess correlation assumed that the scores were sampled from an underlying bivariate normal distribution, requiring that the relationship between the two variables is linear and that the variance of one is the same for any value of the other you might specify (homoscedasticity).

Fortunately, not all assumptions are necessary to the validity of the tests. The two-sample t-tests are fairly robust to deviations from normality, as long as the variances in the two groups are comparable or the design is balanced (Scheffe, 1959). Similarly, the product-moment correlation is fairly robust with respect to the assumption of normality but is sensitive to deviations from the linearity or equal variance assumptions (Kowalski, 1972; Kraemer, 1980).

Measures in the real world often fail to satisfy the assumptions of univariate normality, much less those of bivariate normality. Coffee consumption, for instance, probably has a highly skewed and long-tailed distribution, with some drinking no coffee, the majority of the adult population drinking between one and six cups per day, but a few individuals drinking 10 or 12 or maybe even 20 cups per day. Furthermore, the variance of CMI-A scores is liable to be much greater for the very heavy coffee drinkers than for those with more moderate coffee consumption. To cope with such situations, statisticians frequently recommend *nonparametric tests*, tests that require few assumptions about the underlying distribution of the scores.

If X and Y were both measured on a continuum with few, if any, ties then there is always some transformation of X, say $X^* = f(X)$, and some transformation of Y, say $Y^* = g(Y)$, where X^* and Y^* have normal distributions. However

(X*, Y*) do not necessarily have a bivariate normal distribution (those linearity and homoscedasticity assumptions!). But suppose they did. Then a rank correlation coefficient between X and Y is exactly the same as the rank correlation coefficient between X* and Y*, and the population parameter estimated by the rank correlation coefficient is closely associated with (if not exactly equal to) the ρ_p between X* and Y*. That's the attraction of rank correlation coefficients—we can rescale the X and Y however we wish and the correlation coefficient remains unchanged.

With our worries about the assumptions underlying ρ_p, if we wished to correlate coffee consumption, X, with the CMI-A, Y, we might prefer to use a nonparametric correlation coefficient, such as Kendall's tau (τ) or the Spearman rank correlation (ρ_S) (Fieller et al., 1957; Fieller & Pearson, 1961). Both these tests make no assumptions about the distributions and assume only a monotonic (not necessarily linear) association between the two variables. As above, we consider a correlation of 0.4 to be the critical value, and we wish to determine the sample size required to test $H_0 : \rho_0 = 0$ with 90% power at the 5% level.

For the Spearman rank correlation coefficient,

$$\Delta = (6/\pi) \left[\arcsin (\rho/2) - \arcsin (\rho_0/2)\right]. \tag{5.3.1}$$

$$n = 1.06 \text{ v} + 3.$$

For Kendall's tau,

$$\Delta = (2/\pi) \left[\arcsin (\rho) - \arcsin (\rho_0)\right]. \tag{5.3.2}$$

$$n = 0.437 \text{ v} + 4.$$

Hence, for a one-tailed test at the 5% level with 90% power in our example of coffee consumption and the CMI, where $\rho = 0.4$ and $\rho_0 = 0$ we find $\Delta = 0.38$ and $n = 62$ for the Spearman and $\Delta = 0.26$ and $n = 58$ for the Kendall. If the product-moment correlation coefficient were appropriate, we would have $\Delta = 0.40$ with $n = 51$.

Table 5.3 shows Δ's and corresponding sample sizes for different ρ_p's for the product-moment, the Spearman, and the Kendall coefficients. In every case, nonparametric correlations require a larger sample size than the product-moment correlation, but generally the difference is minimal. Once again, recruiting a few extra subjects is usually a small price to pay to ensure the validity of a study's results. If the parametric assumptions were justified, a point that is often open to question, the researcher will have expended a bit of unnecessary time, effort, and money. On the other hand, if the assumptions on which

Table 5.3 Δ and n^* for Product-Moment Correlation, Spearman Rank Correlation, and Kendall's Tau

	Product-Moment		Spearman		Kendall	
ρ_P	Δ	$n = v + 2$	Δ	$n = 1.06v + 3$	Δ	$n = 0.437v + 4$
0.2	0.2	212	0.19	250	0.13	224
0.3	0.3	93	0.29	107	0.19	106
0.4	0.4	51	0.38	62	0.26	58
0.5	0.5	32	0.48	39	0.33	37
0.6	0.6	21	0.58	26	0.41	25
0.7	0.7	15	0.68	19	0.49	18
0.8	0.8	<10	0.79	<14	0.59	13

*n = sample size required for 90% power at the 5% significance level, one-tailed test.

the parametric test is based were not in fact met, the study will be saved from possibly erroneous conclusions.

Should one prefer the Spearman to the Kendall rank correlation coefficient or vice versa? Clearly from the results of Table 5.3, if ρ_p were valid for (X^*, Y^*), the Spearman coefficient would more closely approximate the Pearson coefficient. If underlying X and Y, there is a continuum, which would certainly be one basis of preferring the Spearman to the Kendall coefficient. However, the Kendall rank correlation coefficient is based on a more general logic than is the Spearman; it is based on doing comparisons between pairs of subjects in the population and is, for that reason, often preferred.

5.4 You Study What You Measure!

To all intents and purposes, nothing we observe is measured on a continuum. While age itself is a continuum, for example, when we record age, we tend to record it accurate to one year for adults (e.g., 35 years of age) and accurate to one month for infants (e.g., 17 months of age). Thus we always group responses (35 means age $\geq$ 35 but age < 36). In any sample of n from a population, there are very likely no ties in true age (no two born at exactly the same instant) but several ties in recorded age.

It has long been known that grouping data biases the estimates of population parameters: the mean, the variance, or any correlation coefficient. How much bias depends on how coarse the grouping, well indicated by how many ties there are in the recorded observations. Thus among adults ranging in age between 20 and 80, grouping by one year would barely affect estimates, while grouping by 20-year intervals (20–39, 40–59, 60–70) might result in a quite different story. The more ties, the more questionable are any statistical tests and estimation procedures based on normality assumptions.

If faced with X and Y with very few ties where exploratory data indicate a monotonic association, the power calculations for the rank correlation coefficients tend to be quite robust. The more ties there are, the more questionable are those calculations, not merely because the underlying assumptions may fail but because grouping data tends to attenuate the population correlation coefficient. The more ties there are, the larger the sample size must be to have adequate power.

To give a vivid demonstration of this fact, consider dichotomization, the most extreme grouping. If the pair (X*, Y*) have a bivariate normal distribution with zero correlation, clearly no dichotomization (or grouping) will induce anything other than a zero correlation. Consider, however, the other extreme shown in Figure 5.4. Here $\rho_p = .9$, and dichotomization is done at the 100Pth percentile of the X* distribution and the 100Qth percentile of the Y* distribution. The maximal possible phi coefficient occurs when both are dichotomized at their medians, in which case the correlation coefficient is reduced from .9 to .71, not a minor decrease. In general, the correlation between dichotomized (X*, Y*) for a fixed P or a fixed Q is largest when P = Q, but the magnitude of that correlation decreases the further this common value is from P = Q = .5. Most worrisome, the correlation coefficient for dichotomized values can actually approach zero if P and Q are very disparate. For example, here when P = .1 and Q = .9 or when P = .9 and Q = .1, the correlation between dichotomized values here is .11 (down from .9!). The price to pay for dichotomization is much, much too great. As many statisticians over the years have suggested, one should never dichotomize ordinal data for purposes of testing or estimation (Cohen, 1983; DeCoster & Iselin, 2009; MacCallum, Zhang, Preacher, & Rucker, 2002; Royston, Altman, & Sauerbrei, 2006).

Indeed, the cost is only slightly less when moving from dichotomization to three- or four-point groupings (e.g., 0: no coffee drinking; 1: moderate coffee drinking, one to five cups per day; 2: heavy coffee drinking, six or more cups per day). Once beyond five or more points on the grouped scale, provided all those points are used relatively frequently (thus reducing the number of ties), the argument against grouping becomes less adamant. Nevertheless, if given a choice between any grouping and using the original ordinal scale for purposes of testing, it would be preferable to use rank correlation methods for the original scales than to group any more than is necessitated by the precision of recording of the data. The same principles apply to group comparisons (t-test, ANOVA) and to any other statistical tests.

Earlier we emphasized and here repeat, the importance of reliability of measures used on the power of tests. When measuring the correlation between two measures, X and Y, where the true measures are ξ and η, it has long been known that the correlation between X and Y is an attenuation of the correlation between ξ and η, the ratio of the true correlation to the observed correlation equal to $\sqrt{\rho_{XX}\rho_{YY}}$, where ρ_{XX} is the reliability coefficient of X and ρ_{YY} the reliability coefficient of Y. Thus if the reliability coefficient (intraclass correlation coefficient) of X is .4 and that of Y is .6, then the observed correlation (product-moment correlation coefficient) between X and Y is 49% of the true correlation between ξ and η. Thus, observed data are always grouped to some extent, but researchers should take warning against any further grouping. After testing is completed, we can always display grouped data in descriptive statistics if that helps the communication of results but only after testing is completed.

Figure 5.4 The pair (X*, Y*) have a bivariate normal distribution with $\rho_P = .9$. Shown is the correlation coefficient (phi) based on dichotomizing X* at the 100Pth percentile and Y* at the 100Qth percentile.

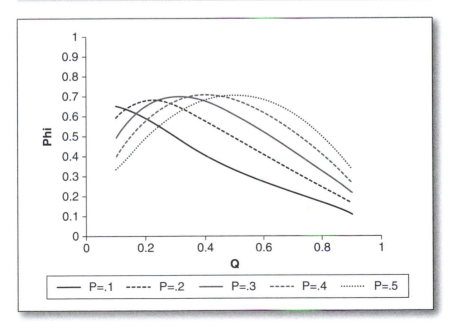

REFERENCES

Cohen, J. (1983). The cost of dichotomization. *Applied Psychological Measurement, 7*(3), 249–253.

DeCoster, J., & Iselin, A.-M. R. (2009). A conceptual and empirical examination of justifications for dichotomization. *Psychological Methods, 14*(4), 349–366.

Fieller, E., Hartley, E. C., & Pearson, E. (1957). Tests for rank correlation coefficients I. *Biometrika*, 44(3,4), 470–481.

Fieller, E., & Pearson, E. S. (1961). Tests for rank correlation coefficients I. *Biometrika*, 48(1,2), 29–40.

Kowalski, C. J. (1972). On the effects on non-normality on the distribution of the sample correlation coefficient. *The Journal of the Royal Statistical Society, 21*, 1–12.

Kraemer, H. C. (1980). Robustness of the distribution theory of the product-moment correlation coefficient. *Journal of Educational Statistics, 5*(2), 115–128.

MacCallum, R. C., Zhang, S., Preacher, K. J., & Rucker, D. D. (2002). On the practice of dichotomization of quantitative variables. *Psychological Methods, 7*(1), 19–40.

Royston, P., Altman, D. G., & Sauerbrei, W. (2006). Dichotomizing continuous predictors in multiple regression: A bad idea. *Statistics in Medicine, 25*, 127–141.

Scheffé, H. (1959). *The analysis of variance.* New York: Wiley.

6

Linear Regression Analysis

I n statistical applications, regression analysis is the process of finding the best mathematical model within a restricted class of models to describe one variable, Y, as a function of one or more other variables, X_1, X_2, ... (Last, 1995). So defined, this includes a huge range of possible analytic methods. The most common regression analysis stipulates that the function is a *linear* combination of p specified variables, that is, $\alpha + \beta_1 X_1 + \beta_2 X_2 + \ldots \beta_p X_p$, and Y is a characteristic or response of a subject sampled from some specified population. This would include not only linear regression analyses (LRA), where Y is an interval-level measure, but also commonly used approaches, such as the logistic regression analysis, where Y is binary (yes/no), or Cox proportional hazards model, where Y is the time to a specified event (a survival time) where some of the times are censored. While the model focuses on obtaining the best fit between a linear combination of the set of Xs to predict Y, many of the uses of such models focus on the individual contributions made by each X in the overall predication, a very different task.

We will focus here on three specific examples of LRAs: a simple linear regression ($p = 1$), a moderator analysis ($p = 3$), and multiple linear regression ($p > 1$). Moreover, we will focus on those issues that have direct relevance to the question *How Many Subjects?* Many of the issues pertinent to LRA also apply to the wider class of linear models and even beyond to general regression analysis.

LRA is very commonly used in biobehavioral research, but it is probably also the most misused, misunderstood, and misinterpreted approach as well. Part of the problem arises from loose terminology. Y is called the dependent variable (DV) or the outcome. The Xs are called the independent variables (IVs) or *covariates* or *predictors*. To call an IV a predictor and the DV the *outcome* is to suggest that the IV precedes the DV in time and perhaps even causes the outcome. Yet in many applications, the IVs measure some characteristic of the subject that may be coincident or may even follow the DV in time and thus can neither predict nor cause. For example, epidemiologists often do cross-sectional studies (each subject measured only at one point of time) with Y indicating the presence or severity of a disorder and the Xs various characteristics of the subject that, if related to Y, are called "risk factors" for that disorder (Kraemer et al., 1997) and often interpreted as if they were causal. If, however, some Xs describe characteristics that are coincident with the disorder, they may be signs or symptoms of the disorder rather than risk factors or predictors for that disorder. If some Xs describe characteristics that follow the onset of the disorder, it may be that X is a result of Y rather than vice versa. To avoid misleading, here we will call Y the DV and the Xs the IVs or covariates, using the terms *predictor, risk factor,* and *outcome* only when the sampling and design of the study warrants use of such terms.

Another more serious problem lies in the fact that all standard regression tests consider the IVs as fixed, not random, and this is often forgotten by users. The error term, ε, is considered random, and as a result, Y is also a random variable. LRA can be used either in an experimental design, where the Xs are set by the researchers, or in an observational design, where the Xs are sampled from some population, but in either case, in standard analyses the Xs are considered fixed, not random.

6.1 Simple Linear Regression

A "simple" linear regression is one in which X is univariate, $p = 1$: $Y_i = \alpha + \beta_1 X_i + \varepsilon_i$, where the index i indicates the subject sampled, and, again, ε_i are independent of each other and of X_i and normally distributed. α is referred to as the "intercept" and β_1 as a "regression coefficient."

It is always good policy in fitting mathematical models to clearly understand the meaning of each parameter estimated. In the case of a simple linear regression, β_1 represents the change in the mean Y for each unit change in X. Thus, for example, if Y were the CMI (a health index) and if X were binary, say males (coded 1) and females (coded 0), β_1 would be the difference between the male and female means of Y. If X were the age of the subject measured in years, then β_1 would be the mean increase in CMI for each year of age; if age were measured in months, then β_1 would be the mean increase in CMI for each month of age.

The intercept α is the mean of CMI when $X = 0$. If Y were the CMI and X were gender (males: 1; females: 0), α would be the mean CMI for females in the population sampled. If scoring were reversed (males: 0; females: 1), α would be the mean CMI for males in the population sampled. Finally if males were coded $+1/2$ and females $-1/2$, then α would be the halfway between the male and female mean CMIs, as it would be if males were coded $-1/2$ and females $+1/2$. In short, how the IVs are coded often changes the meaning of the parameters estimated as well as the results. Generally, we would recommended that, as a default, the coding of a binary variable be $+1/2$ and $-1/2$, because then α would be the same regardless of which subgroup is assigned $+1/2$, and the parameter estimated pertains to the entire population, not just a subgroup.

More serious problems arise when ordinal $X = 0$ is not within the range of the X-values. For example, if the population sampled ranged in age between 20 and 80 and X were age (years since birth), α would be the mean CMI for newborns (age $= 0$). This is logically impossible since the sample provides no information about anyone younger than 20 years of age, and in any case, CMI as a self-report could not be obtained from newborns. To make sense, it would be better to "center" X at some value within the range of Xs, say by substituting $X - 50$ or deviations of X from the mean or the median of the Xs, in fitting the model. How one centers is up to the researcher, but we would recommend as a default that each ordinal X be centered at its mean. How one centers should be stated when reporting results (Kraemer & Blasey, 2004).

For a simple linear regression, how one centers doesn't change inferences about β_1, but with centering at the mean, the intercept would be the mean CMI for the "typical subject," and would have a clear and logical meaning. In simple LRA, the intercept is often ignored and the focus is only on testing whether $\beta_1 = 0$ and on inferences about β_1. The centering (or its absence) doesn't usually cause a problem. However, in more complex regression analyses (as we will see), centering often makes a major difference in interpreting results.

In simple linear regression, there are no assumptions about the distribution of X. X may be binary (male/female), X may be a three-, four-, five-, . . . point interval scale, X may be measured on a continuum (age), and X may or may not have a normal distribution. The crucial assumptions are the linear association between X and Y and the equality of the variance of the error term for different values of X.

The null hypothesis of greatest interest is $H_0: \beta_1 = \beta_0$, with β_0 usually equal to zero. Then if the sample variance of the Xs is $s_X^2 = \Sigma X_i^2/n$ (here considered fixed, a design decision),

$$v = n - 2,$$

$$\delta = (\beta_1 - \beta_0)/\sigma_\varepsilon,$$

$$\Delta = \delta/(\delta^2 + 1/s_X^2)^{1/2}.$$

If X were binary, the $s_X^2 = pq$, where p is the proportion of the sample of n subjects with one response, and q, with the other. This test is exactly equivalent to the two-sample t-test.

Suppose that (X, Y) were a sample from a bivariate normal distribution with population correlation ρ_P. Recall that for the product-moment correlation for the null hypothesis H_0: $\rho_P = 0$, $\Delta = \rho$, and $\nu = n - 2$. In the regression model, using properties of the bivariate normal distribution

$$\beta = \rho \sigma_Y / \sigma_X,$$

$$\sigma_\varepsilon^2 = (1 - \rho^2)\sigma_Y^2,$$

and s_x^2 would estimate σ_X^2.

When we substitute these values in the formula for Δ for a simple LRA, we find

$$\delta = \beta / \sigma_\varepsilon \approx \rho / [s_X(1 - \rho^2)^{1/2}].$$

Then $\Delta = \delta / (\delta^2 + 1/s_X^2)^{1/2} \approx \rho$.

Because $n = \nu + 2$ for regression as well, we see that in this situation, the answer to *How Many Subjects?* will be the same whether testing the null hypothesis for the regression coefficient or for the Pearson correlation coefficient, although the accuracy of the approximations will differ. However, if the Xs are not normally distributed, the connection between the Pearson correlation coefficient and the linear regression coefficient is severed. One may still use LRA, which makes no assumptions about the distribution of X and considers them fixed, but not the Pearson *r*, which assumes that X is normally distributed and random, not fixed.

6.2 Experimental Design: Choosing the X-values

Because LRA makes no assumptions about the distribution of X and considers them fixed, a researcher can choose to allocate the Xs rather than to sample the Xs and, by doing so, increase power without increasing sample size. Suppose, for example, we hypothesized that a subject's CMI (Y) is a linear function of his coffee consumption (X). We assume, for each subject *i*, that $Y = \alpha + \beta_1 X + \varepsilon$, where the errors are independently normally distributed with mean 0 and variance σ_ε^2.

Now, the researcher might propose to obtain CMIs only from an equal number of subjects who drank no coffee at all (X = 0) and of those who drank nine cups per day (X = 9) or from an equal number of subjects who drank no coffee, one cup per day, two cups, three, four, five, and so forth, up to nine or only from subjects who drank three, four, five, or six cups per day, obtaining an equal number at each of these fixed X-values. These designs appear in Table 6.2.1. These decisions about the spacing of the Xs have considerable impact on the power of the design, because s_x^2 ranges from $s_x^2 = 20.25$ when all the observations are taken at $X = 0$ and $X = 9$ to $s_x^2 = 1.25$, when all the observations are between $X = 3$ and $X = 6$.

Table 6.2.2 shows the Δs for these three designs for values of δ ranging from 0.1 to 1. In every case, the values of the Δ are maximal when half the observations are taken from each end of the scale, while the Δs based on Xs sampled only from the middle of the scale are the smallest and those based on sampling all the Xs are intermediate. Thus, a one-tailed test at the 5% level with

Table 6.2.1 Proportions of Sample Taken at Each Possible X-value in Three Different Designs

	X = 0	1	2	3	4	5	6	7	8	9	s_x^2
Design 1	.5	–	–	–	–	–	–	–	–	.5	20.25
Design 2	.1	.1	.1	.1	.1	.1	.1	.1	.1	.1	8.25
Design 3	–	–	–	.25	.25	.25	.25	–	–	–	1.25

Table 6.2.2 Δ for Different Fixed X-values in Linear Regression*

$\delta = \beta/\sigma$	Design 1	Design 2	Design 3
0.1	0.41	0.28	0.11
0.2	0.67	0.50	0.22
0.3	0.80	0.65	0.32
0.4	0.87	0.75	0.41
0.5	0.91	0.82	0.49
0.6	0.94	0.86	0.56
0.7	0.95	0.90	0.62
0.8	0.96	0.92	0.67
0.9	0.97	0.93	0.71
1.0	0.98	0.94	0.75

*In all cases, an equal number of observations are taken at each X-value sampled.

90% power and $\delta = 0.3$ would require fewer than 10 subjects if the observations were taken only at $X = 0$ and $X = 9$ (five at each value) but 81 subjects if the observations were spread evenly between $X = 3$ and $X = 6$ (say, 21 at each value) and 18 subjects if the observations were spread evenly between $X = 0$ and $X = 9$ (say, two at each value).

But choosing the design with the greatest statistical power is not always the wisest strategy, because power may be gained at the cost of validity. In this case, the model assumes that CMI is a linear function of coffee drinking; but with only two values of coffee drinking (zero and nine cups per day), it would be impossible to document the validity of this assumption if it were to be questioned. Moreover, such a design might be very difficult to implement, since finding people at the extremes, zero cups or nine cups per day, might be very difficult. Sampling only from the middle of the range of possible X (three, four, five, six) values presents a slightly different problem. With this design, we may be able to document that CMI shows at least an approximate linear relation to coffee consumption for between three and six cups of coffee per day, but we have no way of generalizing beyond these values, to either lesser or greater amounts of coffee. Only by sampling the full range of X-values of interest can we draw general conclusions. Furthermore, the wider the range of X-values sampled, the larger s_x^2 and hence the larger the Δ.

There has long been argument about whether it is better to use correlation than regression or vice versa. Clearly if Xs are set by experimental design or otherwise not representative of the Xs in some bivariate distribution in the population, correlation analysis cannot validly be applied. Correlation is based on sampling (X, Y) from a bivariate distribution in some population. However, if (X, Y) are sampled from some bivariate distribution, then there is a legitimate option between regression and correlation analyses. It is somewhat easier to set critical values for the correlation test than for the regression test, and the computations for power are more accurate for the correlation test than for the regression test, but the choice remains. However, the argument often does not pit correlation versus regression but experimental studies versus observational studies. Whichever serves the research needs better should be chosen, and the choice for a simple LRA will have little effect on the answer to *How Many Subjects?*

6.3 A Simple Linear Moderation Example

What if $p > 1$, a multiple (or multivariate) linear regression analysis (MLRA)? Let us begin slowly by considering the problem of detecting a moderator of treatment outcome in a randomized clinical trial (RCT) (Baron & Kenny, 1986;

Kraemer, Frank, & Kupfer, 2006) using a linear model. This is about as simple a MLRA as there is and thus can be used to clearly identify the problems one is likely to encounter with more complex MLRA.

In an RCT, n patients are to be sampled from some population and randomly assigned to two treatment groups (T: T1 and T2, np to T1 and nq to T2) and then treated, and an outcome (Y) is to be evaluated blinded to treatment group membership. A "moderator" of treatment response is some baseline variable (thus uncorrelated with T because of randomization) that identifies subgroups of the population sampled in which the effect of treatment (T1 vs T2) differs. For example, gender moderates the effect of treatment if T1 is more effective than T2 for men but T2 is more effective for women. Because of randomization, if choice of treatment, T, is correlated with treatment outcome Y, it would be appropriate to call T a "risk factor" for Y, and T may well be a "cause" of Y.

The most common model to document moderation in an RCT is an MLRA of the form ($p = 3$: $X_1 = T$, $X_2 = X$, $X_3 = TX$):

$$Y = \alpha + \beta_1 T + \beta_2 X + \beta_3 TX + \varepsilon.$$

Once again, α is the intercept, and the βs are regression coefficients. Often β_1 is called the simple or "main effect of treatment," β_2 the simple or "main effect of X," and β_3 the "two-way (or first order) interaction between T and X." In general, main effects involve only one X, interactions are products of two or more Xs.

Centering is now an essential consideration. To show the impact of lack of centering here, suppose that the two treatments were coded 1 and 0, and X was coded as age (years from birth)—which is unfortunately often done. As stated above, α would be the mean Y for newborns in whichever treatment group was coded 0. β_1 would be the effect of treatment on newborns (X = 0). If the age range of subjects were 20 to 80, neither α nor β_1 would be at all meaningful. Then also β_2 would be the slope of Y on X for those in whichever treatment was coded 0, and might be quite different if one reversed the coding of the treatment groups. Only the meaning of β_3 would be uncompromised, the difference between the slope of Y on X in the two treatment groups. What is remarkable and disturbing is how often this is done, and β_1 is reported as the "treatment effect controlling for age," when it is in fact the treatment effect at best for a subgroup (whichever is coded 0) and sometimes for a nonexistent subgroup!

If, as recommended, we use centered coding and code binary T with +1/2 for T1 and −1/2 for T2 and X as deviations from the sample mean (M = 0 for both groups), then α is the average of the two treatment means for the "typical subject" at the mean of X. β_1 indicates the treatment effect for the "typical subject," β_2 is the average of the two slopes of Y on X in the two treatment groups, and β_3 is the difference between those two slopes:

- Then if $\beta_2 = \beta_3 = 0$, both lines in Figure 6.3 would be flat. Then X is not predictive of Y in either treatment group (both slopes are zero), and X *is* "irrelevant to treatment response." In this case the overall effect of treatment (ignoring X) is exactly the same as the effect of treatment for not only the typical subject but for all subjects regardless of what their value of X.
- If $\beta_2 \neq 0$ but $\beta_3 = 0$, the two lines (as in Figure 6.3) would be parallel. The effect of treatment for the typical subjects (indicated by the vertical distance between the two lines at the mean) is exactly the same as the effect of treatment for any subjects regardless of what X is (the vertical distance for any value of X). Then X is a "nonspecific predictor of Y." In this case, the overall effect of treatment (that ignoring X) is not the same as the effect of treatment in any subgroup defined by a common value of X, because a portion of the overall effect of treatment reflects the influence of X rather than T on Y.
- Finally if $\beta_3 \neq 0$, then, as is true in Figure 6.3, the two response lines are not parallel and may even cross. Then the effect of treatment changes depending on what X is and can even change direction if the two lines cross within the range of X. Then X is a "moderator of treatment response." Thus X is a moderator of T on Y if and only $\beta_3 \neq 0$. Now not only is the overall effect of treatment not the same as the effect of treatment for the typical subject, but the effect of treatment for the typical subject is not the same as that for subjects in subgroups defined by different values of X.

To test the null hypothesis that $\beta_3 = 0$, with a total sample size n, np randomized to T1 and nq to T2, then

$$\delta = \beta_3 / \sigma_e,$$

Figure 6.3   A Moderator of the Treatment Effect on the Outcome Y

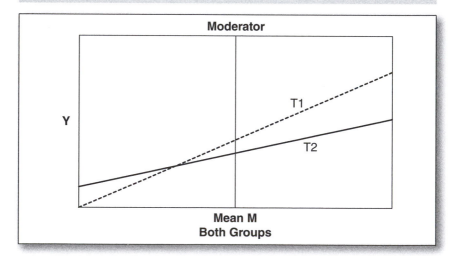

$$\Delta = \delta/(\delta^2 + [1/ps_{x1}^2 + 1/qs_{x2}^2])^{1/2},$$

$$v = n - 4,$$

where s_{x1}^2 and s_{x2}^2 are the sample variances of X (considered fixed) in the T1 and T2 samples.

Because of randomization, in an experimental design, one would expect that the two variances would be approximately the same as the total variance of X in the sample of n subjects, in which case, one might use the overall planned variance of the Xs in the computation. In an observational study, where the Xs are sampled, not set by the researchers, the population variance of X, as indicated by exploratory studies, would be substituted for both variances. If in a balanced design (p = q = 1/2), then

$$\Delta = \delta/(\delta^2 + 4/s_x^2)^{1/2}, \text{ or } \Delta = \delta/(\delta^2 + 4/\sigma_x^2)^{1/2}.$$

6.4 Problems: Collinearity and Interactions

There are two special features to the moderator analysis described above that make this a simple MLR to consider: (a) There are two individual IVs, and their interaction is included; (b) because of randomization, the two IVs are independent. Both of these features simplify the use of MLR in this situation.

Suppose the interaction term had not been included in the model, but the independence still holds. In Figure 6.3 is shown the situation when there is an interaction, two nonparallel lines relating Y to X in T1 and T2. *Omitting the interaction amounts to assuming that these two lines are parallel.* Then in fitting the model, some average (depending on p and q) of the two slopes is computed, and two parallel lines, each with that weighted average of the slopes, are drawn passing through the average Y for the two treatment groups at the mean X. Then β_1 is reported as the "treatment effect controlling for X." Clearly this misrepresents the situation, for that treatment effect β_1 is *only* the treatment effect for the "typical subject," not for subjects with any other value of X.

To make matters worse, when the independence does *not* hold and an existing interaction in the population is omitted in the model, the mean X is then different in the two treatment groups and the so-called "treatment effect controlling for X" may not be the treatment effect for *any* identifiable subgroup of the population. In short, omitting interaction terms in the model when an interaction exists in the population may invalidate all the results of LRA.

However, to include all interactions can pose major problems. When $p = 2$, as above, four parameters are estimated (the intercept, two main effects, and one interaction). When $p = 3$, eight parameters are estimated (the intercept, three main effects, 3 two-way interactions, and 1 three-way interaction). In general with p IVs there are 2^p parameters to be estimated. The greater the number of IVs, the larger the sample size must be for adequate power and the greater the difficulty both in recruiting a sufficient number of subjects and in interpreting the results.

Our recommendation, which is to include interactions unless there is strong rationale and justification not to, is contrary to what often appears in textbooks. Some suggest that interactions should be included only if the interaction itself is of interest. For example, to detect a moderator of treatment where the interaction is the focus, one would include an interaction. However, to detect a mediator of treatment (Sometimes even for the same treatments in the same RCT with the same outcome!), it might be assumed that the interaction is absent. Others suggest that interactions are nuisance variables (And clearly they often are!) and should just be omitted in order to have a clear interpretation of the main effect; although such interpretation might be clear, it may also be wrong. Yet others suggest that the interaction effects, even when they exist, are likely to be so small as not to make much difference. Often this is true, but not always, and when they are not small but are omitted, the results can mislead. We have to disagree: Interactions should be omitted only when there is strong rationale and justification that they do not exist. Otherwise, if there is to be any interpretation of the individual regression coefficients, they should be included. This recommendation, in turn, means that we need to be very parsimonious and careful in choosing how many and which IVs to include in any analysis in which the regression coefficients are to be estimated, tested, and interpreted.

However, if the goal is not to evaluate individual regression coefficients but only to fit a linear model as closely as possible, then interactions can be omitted. If they exist in the population and are ignored in fitting the model, one merely achieves a less accurate fit than is possible. The problem with omitted interactions noted earlier, all occur in the interpretation of individual parameters, not the overall fit of the model.

Another problematic issue is collinearity, when the covariates are correlated, that is, $\Sigma X_1 X_2 \neq 0$ (Xs centered at their means). If two IVs are perfectly correlated, then standard methods to estimate the regression coefficients will not work; computer programs to perform such estimation will simply deliver an error message. This is a Type III error, asking a question with no reasonable answer. However, even when X_1 and X_2 measure the same construct, they are usually not perfectly correlated, for their correlation is attenuated by their unreliabilities, and seldom, if ever, is the reliability of a measure perfect. Then asking the question is still a Type III error, but standard computer programs will deliver some answer, though it will be one that cannot be clearly and accurately interpreted.

If X_1 and X_2 are collinear, then β_1 and β_2 both reflect the influence of whatever X_1 and X_2 have in common, and each also reflects whatever X_1 or X_2 uniquely measures. *Moreover, the power to test each of the individual regression coefficients is more seriously attenuated, the stronger the collinearity of the Xs.* Thus, if power considerations are based on the assumption of noncollinearity, the sample sizes may be grossly underestimated if there is collinearity.

If covariates are set by experimental design, a major factor is to eliminate the possibility of collinearity (using balanced or partially balanced designs). This, too, adds to the gain in power with experimental approaches and consequent decrease in the necessary sample size when basing regression analyses on experimental designs rather than observational studies.

6.5 Multiple Linear Regression

Often a researcher decides to investigate the effect of multiple IVs on the DV. In this case, the regression model assumes that for each subject i

$$Y_i = \alpha + \beta_1 X_{i1} + \beta_2 X_{i2} + \ldots + \beta_p X_{ip} + \text{error}_i$$

where $X_1, X_2, \ldots X_p$ are the p covariates, always considered fixed, and the errors are assumed to be independently normally distributed with mean 0 and variance σ_ε^2. The list of independent variables may include interaction terms (e.g., $X_3 = X_1 X_2$) . One might also define IVs as squares (X_1^2) or cubes (X_2^3) of individual variables, that is, polynomial terms. Which independent variables are included depends on the rationale and justification gleaned from exploratory studies. Again it is important that each individual variable be appropriately centered.

To test the effect of any given predictor variable X_j (H_0: $\beta_j = 0$), a t-test is used with N−p−1 degrees of freedom. For this test

$$\delta = \beta_j / \sigma_\varepsilon,$$

$$n = v + p + 1,$$

$$\Delta = \delta / (\delta^2 + 1/w_j^2)^{1/2}.$$

Here w_j^2 depends on the sample variance of X_j and its collinearity with the other predictor variables. The larger the number of predictor variables, the smaller the variance of X_j. The higher its collinearity with other predictor variables or combinations of them, the smaller the w_j^2. In both these situations, the larger is the sample size necessary for adequate power. Seldom in an observational study is it possible in planning a study to know what w_j^2 will be, even approximately, if there are many covariates.

For this reason again, researchers should select their covariates very parsimoniously and very carefully. Inclusion of a great many covariates (p large) or of any covariates that are closely related to each other (collinearity) will decrease the power to detect any effects at all or necessitate greatly increased sample size. For example, a researcher might be tempted to include race, socioeconomic status, level of education, and family income as predictors, even if the population studied is 90% white and predominantly middle-class. All four of these measures tend to intercorrelate highly in any observational sample, and this population is relatively homogeneous in race and socioeconomic status. Detecting a relationship between the outcome variable and a single one of these variables may require 20 to 50 subjects, but investigating all simultaneously may require 200 to 500 subjects, if it can be done at all. It is far better to reduce all those correlated variables to a single one, say, one socioeconomic index that may take into consideration all four factors, and recognize that any influence found may pertain to all of these factors (and others).

Once again, if there are interactions in the population that are omitted in the model, all the estimation procedures may be biased and the error variance increased. As a result, any inferences about individual regression coefficients may be invalid. The overall message is simple: If the issue is to estimate the influence of individual IVs, choose very few covariates and choose them very carefully.

Again, this goes contrary to what is common practice. Researchers could think that by including many covariates they are being careful, and frequently researchers who choose parsimoniously and carefully are criticized by proposal and paper reviewers for not "controlling" or "adjusting" for all sorts of variables. But to do so results not only in reduced power to detect any effects but the risk of invalid results.

The issue is, again, different if the goal is not to assess the influence of individual covariates on the outcome but to assess the influence of a linear combination (whichever one chosen) to estimate the dependent variable, Y. The usual measure of association is the multiple correlation coefficient, ρ_M, the product-moment correlation coefficient between the observed Y and the Y estimated by the linear combination of the covariates. If the weights (regression coefficients) were prespecified and Y were normally distributed, then in the master tables

$$\Delta = \rho_M,$$

$$v = n - p - 1.$$

If the regression coefficients are estimated in the sample and used to estimate Y and the multiple correlation coefficient tested in the same sample, the same calculation would be used but would be more approximate.

In summary, regression analysis is a useful analytic tool in behavioral sciences research and is the most widely used statistical procedure. The scientific literature contains both examples of its appropriate application and its misuse. Unfortunately, its misuse is not always obvious to the research consumer. It is helpful to remind here that the "predictor" variables are considered fixed (rather than random) in the common application of regression, as described in this chapter. Moreover, fitting the linear model (e.g., the least squares solution, which finds the line of best fit and minimizes the distance from the actual data and the data "predicted" by the regression line) is a separate process that must be distinguished from that of drawing inferences from the statistics for individual Xs (e.g., beta weights and p values). As with all statistical procedures, the application of regression in observational designs and experimental designs has implications. Correlated Xs, while allowed in regression analyses, preclude the ability to estimate power and to interpret the results clearly and accurately. If too highly correlated (collinear), the associations among the Xs will bias all parameter estimates generated from the model. Exclusion of interaction terms can also yield inaccurate regression results (and also ignores some of the most interesting questions that can be answered in the study, e.g., moderation). Lack of centering further contributes to the discrepancy between statistical estimates and population parameters. We urge researchers to be aware of these issues and to communicate their models, including the intercorrelations among the IVs and the centered coding procedures, to the reader so that proper inferences can be made.

REFERENCES

Baron, R. M., & Kenny, D. A. (1986). The moderator-mediator variable distinction in social psychological research: Conceptual, strategic, and statistical considerations. *Journal of Personality and Social Psychology, 51,* 1173–1182.

Kraemer, H. C., & Blasey, C. (2004). Centring in regression analysis: A strategy to prevent errors in statistical inference. *International Journal of Methods in Psychiatric Research, 13*(3), 141–151.

Kraemer, H. C., Frank, E., & Kupfer, D. J. (2006). Moderators of treatment outcomes: Clinical, research, and policy importance. *Journal of the American Medical Association, 296*(10), 1–4.

Kraemer, H. C., Kazdin, A. E., Offord, D. R., Kessler, R. C., Jensen, P. S., & Kupfer, D. J. (1997). Coming to terms with the terms of risk. *Archives of General Psychiatry, 54,* 337–343.

Last, J. M. (1995). *A dictionary of epidemiology.* New York: Oxford University.

7

Homogeneity of Variance Tests

Just as researchers might wish to compare two means, so too might they be interested in comparing two variances. Often a condition or treatment will not systematically affect the means of the variables of interest, but individual differences between subject responses may be greater with one treatment than another, an increase in variance. Or quite commonly, two measures of the same quantity will have essentially the same mean, but one will show much greater error variance than the other. This chapter discusses tests appropriate for such situations.

7.1 Two Independent Samples

Suppose that, with a total sample size of n, we sample a proportion p subjects from one population and a proportion q from another ($p + q = 1$) and measure a variable known to be normally distributed in both populations. To test whether the variance of the first sample (σ_x^2) is greater than that of the second sample (σ_y^2), we compare the ratio of the variances with the F-value at $np - 1$ and $nq - 1$ degrees of freedom. Here the effect size would be Λ, where

$$\Delta = (\sigma_x^2 - \sigma_y^2)/(\sigma_x^2 + \sigma_y^2) \tag{7.1}$$

$$n = [(v+3) + [(v+3)^2 - 16pq(v+2)]^{1/2}]/4pq$$

For instance, even though physician-interview and self-report CMI scores may not differ in terms of their means, one method may yield scores with much smaller variance than the other. In such a situation, we would prefer the score with smaller variance, because the power of a test is always decreased by increased within-group variance.

For example, in the two-sample t-test comparing the two means, with $p = q = 0.5$,

$$\Delta = \delta/(\delta^2 + 4)^{1/2} \text{ and } n = v + 2,$$

where δ is the difference between the two means divided by the pooled within-group standard deviation. Now, if the variance were doubled, δ would decrease by a factor of $2^{1/2}$, and we would have, in terms of the original δ,

$$\Delta = \delta / (\delta^2 + 8)^{1/2}.$$

This means, for example, that doubling the variance would decrease Δ from 0.45 to 0.33 for $\delta = 1$. Thus, instead of 40 subjects, a one-tailed test at the 5% level with 90% power would require approximately 77 subjects. Choosing the measure with the smaller variance, in other words, cuts the necessary sample size for a t-test almost in half.

With these facts in mind, we might design a small study to compare the variances of physician-interview and self-report CMI scores, sampling a total of n subjects, randomly assigning them to two groups, one in which scores are obtained by self-report (a proportion p of the total sample) and the remaining (a proportion q) for which the scores are obtained by physician interview. Let us say that the standard deviation of the self-report scores is known to be approximately 6 ($\sigma_x = 6$) from previous work, so the variance is approximately 36 ($\sigma_x^2 = 36$). If the variance of the physician interview scores were half that or approximately 18 ($\sigma_y^2 = 18$), we would consider using these in future studies, even though they are substantially more expensive to obtain. Thus, the critical value is

$$\Delta = (\sigma_x^2 - \sigma_y^2) / (\sigma_x^2 + \sigma_y^2) = (36 - 18) / (36 + 8) = 0.33$$

The important design decision in this study, just as with the two-sample t-test, is the choice of the proportions p and q. When $p = q = 0.5$, the formula for n simplifies to $(2v+4)$.

Thus, for 90% power at the 5% level

$$n = 2(75) + 4 = 154.$$

When $p = 0.9$ and $q = 0.1$, on the other hand, calculations yield

$$n = \frac{(75+3) + [(75+3)^2 - 16(0.9)(0.1)(75+2)]^{1/2}}{4(0.9)(0.1)} \approx 432$$

Table 7.2.1 gives more information on the effect of imbalance on necessary sample size for selected values of v and p. As in the case of t-tests, mild imbalance has little impact, but extremely imbalanced groups (say p or $q \geq 0.75$) will require significantly more subjects than a balanced design to achieve the same power. As with the t-test, power is maximized, and therefore sample size is minimized at $p = 0.5$.

7.2 Matched Samples

Rather than using two independent samples of subjects to test the hypothesis that self-report and physician-interview CMI scores have the same variance (cross-sectional study), we might choose to study one set of subjects, with each individual subject within the set observed under both conditions, presented in random order, and separated by some time to avoid carry-over effects, using the same sort of repeated-measures design we used for the matched-pairs t-test. The test in this case, developed by (Morgan, 1939; Pitman, 1939), has the effect size Δ, where

$$\Delta = (\sigma_x^2 - \sigma_y^2)/[(\sigma_x^2 + \sigma_y^2)^2 - 4\rho^2\sigma_x^2\sigma_y^2]^{1/2} \qquad (7.2)$$

Table 7.2.1   Sample Sizes for Varying Degrees of Imbalance in the Two-Group Variance-Ratio Test

	p, q=				
v	0.5	0.6, 0.4	0.7, 0.3	0.8, 0.2	0.9, 0.1
20	44	46	53	70	126
30	64	67	77	102	182
40	84	88	101	133	237
50	104	109	125	164	293
60	124	130	148	195	349
70	144	151	172	227	404
80	164	171	196	258	460
90	184	192	220	289	515
100	204	213	244	320	571

Table 7.2.2 Values of Δ for Differing Values of the Variance Ratio (σ_x^2 / σ_y^2) and Correlation (ρ) Between Responses in the Matched Sample Test

ρ = (σ_x^2 / σ_y^2)	0.00	0.1	0.2	0.3	0.4	0.5	0.6	0.7	0.8	0.9
1.00	0.00	0.00	0.00	0.00	0.00	0.00	0.00	0.00	0.00	0.00
1.25	0.11	0.11	0.11	0.12	0.12	0.13	0.14	0.15	0.18	0.25
1.50	0.20	0.20	0.20	0.21	0.22	0.23	0.25	0.27	0.32	0.42
2.00	0.33	0.33	0.34	0.35	0.36	0.38	0.40	0.44	0.51	0.63
2.50	0.43	0.43	0.44	0.45	0.46	0.48	0.51	0.55	0.62	0.74
3.00	0.50	0.50	0.51	0.52	0.53	0.55	0.59	0.63	0.69	0.80
4.00	0.60	0.60	0.61	0.62	0.63	0.65	0.68	0.72	0.78	0.86
6.00	0.71	0.72	0.72	0.73	0.74	0.76	0.79	0.82	0.86	0.92
9.00	0.80	0.80	0.81	0.81	0.82	0.84	0.86	0.88	0.91	0.95
20.00	0.90	0.91	0.91	0.91	0.92	0.93	0.94	0.95	0.96	0.98
100.00	0.98	0.98	0.98	0.98	0.98	0.99	0.99	0.99	0.99	1.00

$n = v + 2$, where σ_x^2 is the variance of the first measure, σ_y^2 that of the second and ρ the correlation between the two.

To continue the example above, suppose the correlation between physician-interview and self-report scores was 0.5 ($\rho = .5$), and the variance of the physician scores is still 18 ($\sigma_y^2 = 18$), while that of the self-report scores is 36 ($\sigma_x^2 = 36$). Then

$$\Delta = (36 - 18) / [(36+18)^2 - (4)(0.5)^2(36)(18)]^{1/2} = 0.38,$$

$$n = 55 + 2 = 57$$

for 90% power at the 5% significance level. Here, we require 57 subjects each measured twice (114 observations) rather than 154 subjects each measured once (154 subjects and observations), when we proposed to use independent (unmatched) groups and a balanced design.

The power of the matched design increases with the degree of correlation between paired responses (ρ). Table 7.2.2 shows the effect on Δ of an increasing correlation coefficient between the two scores. When the correlation is zero, the scores are independent, and this design is equivalent to the two-group (unmatched) design with equal group sizes, except that only half as many subjects ($v + 2$ rather than $2v + 4$) are required, because each subject is measured twice. If recruiting subjects is difficult, then feasibility considerations alone will argue for a matched design. If the correlation between the scores is even moderately strong, then the matched design offers significantly more power as well, and in such situations, the Morgan-Pitman test statistic will generally be preferred to the more familiar variance-ratio F-test.

In sum, statistical power for comparing variances is optimized under some of the same conditions that maximize statistical power for tests that compare means. Comparisons of variances for two groups with comparable sample sizes have greater power than comparisons of groups with highly imbalanced sample sizes. Matched pairs designs can increase statistical power, and the amount of power increases the larger the correlation between the paired observations.

REFERENCES

Morgan, W. A. (1939). A test for the significance of the difference between the two variances in a sample from a normal bivariate population. *Biometrika, 31*, 13–19.

Pitman, E. J. G. (1939). A note on normal correlation. *Biometrika, 31*, 9–12.

8

Binomial Tests

A ll the tests discussed thus far have been based on measurements that can at least be ordered. In fact, except for nonparametric correlation, we have assumed not only ordinal measures but also that some underlying distributions were normal. Research, however, often concerns nominal level variables, variables resulting from categories that cannot even be ordered, far less considered normally distributed. Gender, race, and religious affiliation are examples of such variables. This chapter discusses tests appropriate for dichotomous variables, like gender, with only two values.

8.1 Single-Sample Binomial Tests

Because dichotomous variables can assume only two values, questions about them concern not their means but the proportion of the sample assuming each value. Just as the one-sample t-test can be used either to compare the mean of a single measurement with some specified value or to detect a difference between the means of paired scores (matched-pairs t-test), so can the one-sample binomial be used either to compare the proportions in a sample with some specified value (usually 0.5) or to detect a difference in paired values.

For convenience, call the two values of the variable "yes" and "no" and let π be the population proportion of "yes" responses we consider it important to detect, while π_0 is the proportion specified under the null hypothesis. Then, to use the master table

$$\delta = 2 \, (\arcsin \pi^{1/2} - \arcsin \pi_0^{1/2}), \qquad (8.1.1)$$

$$\Delta = (e^{2\delta} - 1) / (e^{2\delta} + 1),$$

$$n = v - 1.$$

Suppose, for example, that instead of some scaled measure of health like the CMI, we had only information about whether the subject sought medical treatment (other than a routine physical) in the past year (yes) or not (no). We wish to discover whether the proportion of those seeking treatment was higher among coffee drinkers than in the general population. Suppose we decide to sample coffee drinkers in their fifties, reasoning that their exposure to coffee has been sufficient to affect their health (if it does), and wish to detect an increase of 10% in the proportion seeking medical care with 90% power at the 5% level of significance. If the proportion of the general population in their fifties seeking medical treatment is known to be 0.5 (π_0 = 0.5) then for a 10% increase (π = .6):

$$\delta = 2\,(\arcsin 0.6^{1/2} - \arcsin 0.5^{1/2}) = 0.20,$$

$$\Delta = (e^{2\delta} - 1) / (e^{2\delta} + 1) = 0.20,$$

$$n = v - 1 = 209.$$

There are several versions of this test in common use under different names. The equivalent of the matched-pairs t-test for a dichotomous (yes/no) variable is called McNemar's test (Siegel, 1956). In this test, all tied pairs (i.e., yes-yes or no-no) are discarded, and a single-sample binomial is used to test whether the proportion of yes-no pairs equals the proportion of no-yes pairs (i.e., π_0 = .5). Here π is the yes-no proportion among untied pairs and γ the proportion of untied pairs. Then

$$\delta = 2\,[(\arcsin \pi^{1/2} - \arcsin 0.5^{1/2})], \tag{8.1.2}$$

$$\Delta = (e^{2\delta} - 1) / (e^{2\delta} + 1),$$

$$n = (v - 1) / \gamma.$$

If half the subjects are expected to give the same response both times ($\gamma = 0.50$), in other words, then $2(v - 1)$ subjects must be sampled to achieve the specified power, while if 75% respond the same way both times ($\gamma = 0.25$), then $n = 4(v - 1)$. Thus, McNemar's test can require extremely large sample sizes if used with highly correlated responses that produce small values of γ.

The sign test (Siegel, 1956) and the single-sample median test are also special applications of the single-sample binomial test, in which observations are dichotomized as yes or no according to whether they satisfy some ordering or not. For instance, in the single-sample median test, scores may be dichotomized as to whether they fall above or below a median specified in the null hypothesis.

Suppose, for example, we wished to test whether the mean μ of some normally distributed variable with variance σ^2 were in fact zero. Since the mean equals the median in a normal distribution, we could either use the single-sample t-test, or we could dichotomize the data, denoting all positive values as yes and all negative values as no, and testing whether there were approximately equal numbers of positive and negative scores ($\pi_0 = 0.5$) with the single-sample binomial test. Both would be valid tests. Recall that for the one-sample t-test (4.1)

$$\delta = \mu/\sigma,$$

$$\Delta = \delta / (\delta^2 + 1)^{1/2},$$

$$n = v + 1.$$

For the binomial test (8.1) in this situation we have

$$\pi = \Phi(\mu/\sigma) = \Phi(\delta),$$

where Φ is the cumulative standard normal distribution function, and

$$\delta = 2[\arcsin \pi^{1/2} - \arcsin 0.5^{1/2}],$$

$$\Delta = (e^{2\delta} - 1) / (e^{2\delta} + 1),$$

$$n = v - 1.$$

Table 8.2.1 shows the relationship of π to $\delta = \mu / \sigma$ and the corresponding Δs for the binomial and t-tests. In every case, the Δ for the binomial test is smaller than that for the t-test: More subjects would be required to achieve the same power. For instance, if $\delta = 0.1$, for a one-tailed test at the 5% level with 90% power, we have for the t-test

$$\Delta = 0.10,$$

$$n = 852 + 1 = 853,$$

and for the binomial,

$$\Delta = 0.08,$$

$$n = 1334 - 1 = 1333,$$

a difference of almost 500 subjects. How the response is measured, whether on a continuum or dichotomized, can make a significant difference in the power of the test. The researcher must consider whether the greater ease of using a dichotomy instead of a continuous variable outweighs the effort and expense of studying this many more subjects (Cohen, 1983).

8.2 Two-Sample Binomial Test

Like the t-test, the binomial can be used both to compare the scores of one sample to some specified value, as discussed above, and to compare the scores of two samples with each other. In the two-sample case, if the total sample size is n, and we sample a fraction p from one group and a fraction q from a second $(p + q = 1)$, then, to use the master table,

$$\delta = 2\,(pq)^{1/2}\,(\arcsin \pi_x^{1/2} - \arcsin\pi_y^{1/2}),\qquad(8.2)$$

$$\Delta = (e^{2\delta} - 1) / (e^{2\delta} + 1),$$

$$n = v - 1,$$

where π_x and π_y are the proportions of yes response in the two groups.

Table 8.2.1   Comparison of Δ for Single-Sample t-test and Single-Sample Binomial

$\delta = \mu/\sigma$	π^*	Δ for t	Δ for **Binomial**
0.1	0.54	0.10	0.08
0.2	0.58	0.20	0.16
0.3	0.62	0.29	0.23
0.4	0.66	0.37	0.31
0.5	0.69	0.45	0.37
0.6	0.73	0.51	0.44
0.7	0.76	0.57	0.49
0.8	0.79	0.62	0.55
0.9	0.82	0.67	0.59
1.0	0.84	0.71	0.64

$^*\pi = \Phi(\delta)$ where Φ is the cumulative standard normal distribution function.

Suppose, for example, that instead of comparing the proportion of coffee drinkers in their fifties seeking medical care to that of the hypothetical general population, we chose to compare coffee drinkers with abstainers, again using a 10% difference as the critical effect size we wish to detect with 90% power at the 5% significance level. As with the two-sample t-test and the independent-group variance ratio test, power is maximized with a balanced $(p = q = 0.5)$ design and will be severely diminished with very unbalanced $(p \geq 0.75$, roughly$)$ group sizes. We therefore choose $p = q = 0.5$ and use as our estimate of π_y (the proportion of coffee abstainers seeking medical care), the proportion of the general population of subjects in their fifties who seek medical care, known from previous studies to be about 0.5 $(\pi_y = .5)$. Hence for a 10% increase $(\pi_x = .6)$,

$$\delta = 2\,((0.5)\,(0.5))^{1/2}\,[(\arcsin 0.6^{1/2} - \arcsin 0.5^{1/2})] = 0.1$$

$$\Delta = (e^{0.2} - 1)\,/\,(e^{0.2} + 1) = 0.1$$

$$n = v - 1 = 852 - 1 = 851,$$

meaning approximately 426 subjects per group are required for 90% power.

As noted above, researchers sometimes choose to dichotomize a continuous variable. In such a situation, a two-sample binomial might be used instead of the two-sample t-test. If, for example, a variable is normally distributed with mean μ_x in one group and mean μ_y in the second group, both having a common variance σ^2, then the t-test could be used with

$$\delta = (\mu_x - \mu_y)\,/\,\sigma$$

$$\Delta = \delta\,/\,(\delta^2 + 1/pq)^{1/2},$$

$$n = v + 2.$$

On the other hand, if the variable were dichotomized at point $\bar{\mu} + C\sigma$, where the $\bar{\mu}$ is the average of the two group means, then

$$\pi_x = \Phi\,(C + \delta/2), \pi_y = \Phi(C - \delta/2),$$

and the two-sample binomial could be used with

$$\delta = 2\,(pq)^{1/2}\,[\arcsin \pi_x^{1/2} - \arcsin \pi_y^{1/2}],$$

$$\Delta = (e^{2\delta)} - 1)\,/\,(e^{2\delta)} + 1),$$

$$n = v - 1.$$

Table 8.2.2 shows the effect of varying the cut-off value (C) for different values of $\delta = (\mu_x - \mu_y)/\sigma$. In every case, the critical effect size for the binomial test is smaller than that for the t-test. When the cut-off is halfway between the two group means (C = 0), the effect size is largest, but even then there is some loss.

How serious the problems can be is better seen in Table 8.2.3, where the example considered in Chapter 4 for the two-sample t-test is reconsidered. In that example, we saw that when $\delta = .5$, and seeking 80% power for a 5% one-tailed test, we needed 107 subjects for a balanced or near-balanced design, but as many as 274 subjects with a 90 to 10 split in group sizes (see t-test column in Table 8.2.3). As one dichotomizes at various cut-off points (C), the sample size increases to 2469. The discrepancy between 107 and 2469 subjects is far from trivial and should cause a researcher to pause and consider whether the ease of using dichotomous response instead of a continuous response is worth the effort and expense of studying so many more subjects (Cohen, 1983).

Some research questions are tested using dichotomous or binary variables (e.g. male and female, responder and nonresponder). Using statistical tests to answer research questions that include such binary measurements will require substantially more subjects to achieve sufficient statistical power.

Table 8.2.2   Critical Effect Sizes (Δ) for a Balanced Two-Sample t-test and Binomial Test With Different Points of Dichotomization

	Binomial Test					T-test
δ	C: ± 2	± 1.5	± 1	± 0.5	0	Δ for t
0.1	0.02	0.03	0.03	0.04	0.04	0.05
0.2	0.04	0.05	0.07	0.08	0.08	0.10
0.3	0.05	0.08	0.10	0.11	0.12	0.15
0.4	0.07	0.10	0.13	0.15	0.16	0.20
0.5	0.09	0.13	0.16	0.19	0.20	0.24
0.6	0.11	0.15	0.20	0.22	0.23	0.29
0.7	0.13	0.18	0.23	0.26	0.27	0.33
0.8	0.14	0.20	0.26	0.29	0.31	0.37
0.9	0.16	0.23	0.29	0.33	0.34	0.41
1	0.18	0.25	0.32	0.36	0.37	0.45

Table 8.2.3   Sample Size Necessary for 80% Power to Detect $\delta = .5$ Using a One-Tailed 5% Test With the t-test and With the Binomial Test for Balanced (p, $q = .5$) and Unbalanced Designs and Various Cutoffs (C) for Dichotomizing $\delta = .5$ Responses

| p, q | t-test | Binomial Test | | | | |
		C: 0.0	0.5	1.0	1.5	2.0
0.1	274	426	507	615	962	2469
0.2	154	238	271	362	615	1258
0.3	127	187	210	271	426	962
0.4	107	168	187	238	362	760
0.5	107	151	168	238	362	760

As demonstrated, splitting an ordinal or continuous measure into two groups (e.g., converting CESD depression scores in high and low groups) is a costly decision and will require recruitment and participation of many subjects. Despite these warnings, clinical researchers are sometimes tempted to create "groups" from continuous variables rather than utilize the variables in their original continuous format.

This chapter underscores that continuous measure, if available, should never be converted to binary variables for the purposes of hypothesis testing. After testing the hypothesis using a continuous variable, the researcher may choose to dichotomize or create groups—only for descriptive or illustrative purposes.

REFERENCES

Cohen, J. (1983). The cost of dichotomization. *Applied Psychological Measurement, 7*(3), 249–253.

Siegel, S. (1956). *Non-parametric statistics for the behavioral sciences*. New York: McGraw-Hill

9

Contingency Table Analysis

O ne of the easiest and most common of statistical tests is the I by J contingency table χ^2-test. Unfortunately, it is also one of the most difficult tests for which to plan and, in addition, one of the very weakest of tests. For this test, each of a sample of n subjects is classified into unordered categories X1, X2, ... XI and unordered categories Yl, Y2, ...YJ, the data summarized in an I by J table (Table 9.0). To test the association (correlation, dependency) between X and Y, a statistic is computed and referred to the χ^2-table with $(I - 1)(J - 1)$ degrees of freedom. A number of issues must be considered.

First of all, the test statistic can validly be referred to the χ^2-table only if the sample is large enough to yield a reasonable number in each marginal position (np_i and nq_j). There is no general agreement as to how large is "reasonable." One of the more common rules of thumb is that

$$np_i q_j \geq 5 \text{ for each } i \text{ and } j.$$

One or more rare categories (e.g., $p_i = 0.05$, $q_j = 0.1$) will necessitate a large *minimal* sample size (e.g., $n (0.05)(0.1) \geq 5$ means $n \geq 1000$) to use the test at all, even before power is at issue. With an I by J table, the minimal total sample size under any conditions is therefore 5IJ (i.e., $(5)(3)(4) = 60$ for a 3 by 4 table).

Second, there are a variety of possible sampling plans. A representative sample of size n may be drawn from some population with responses falling where they may in the I by J table: *naturalistic sampling*. In that case, $p_1, p_2, \ldots p_i$ and $q_1, q_2, \ldots q_j$ estimate the probability distributions of X and Y in the population. This is generally what occurs in an observational study.

Alternatively, the researchers may select proportions $p_1, p_2, \ldots p_i$ in each X-category and let the Y-responses in each row fall where they may: *X-stratified sampling*. Or they may select proportions $q_1, q_2, \ldots q_j$ in each Y-category and let the X-responses in each column fall where they may: *Y-stratified sampling*. In each of the stratified cases, the p$_i$'s and q$_j$'s reflect design decisions and cannot be used to estimate population characteristics. Because one can stratify to avoid rare categories, stratified sampling usually yields more power to detect association than does naturalistic sampling. This is generally what occurs in an experimental designed study.

There is another theoretical option in which all row and column proportions are set by the researcher. We have never seen such a sampling plan used, nor can we envision how it could be used. However, when Fisher's exact test is used to test the hypothesis, that sampling plan is what is assumed. The assumption has no effect on the validity of the null test but precludes any a priori considerations of power considerations. Many statisticians routinely recommend against using the Fisher's exact test for a variety of reasons, as we do here (Lyderson, Fagerland, & Laake, 2009).

Third, this test is designed for use when the X and Y categories are unordered. When either X or Y is ordered, this test remains valid but is far less powerful than other valid nonparametric tests that capitalize on the ordering (rank correlations for naturalistic sampling, Mann-Whitney, Kruskal-Wallis for experimental designs).

What we suggest for power calculation is this: We dissect the full I by J table into IJ 2 by 2 tables. For each pair of X and Y categories, we decide whether or not that particular association is important to detect. If it is important, we decide how strong an association it is critical to detect and base power calculations on that decision.

9.1 The I by J χ^2-test

For each X_i and Y_j whose association we consider important, we reduce the I by J table to a 2 by 2 table (Table 9.1). In naturalistic sampling, p_i and q_j are the probabilities of observing X_i and Y_j; in X-stratified samples p_i is the proportion of the sample the researcher has decided to obtain and q_j the proportion of Y_j

Table 9.0   An I by J Contingency Table

	Y1	Y2 . . . YJ	
X1			np_1
X2			np_2
XI			np_1
	$n_{1'}$	$nq_2 . . . nq_j$	

that result; and in Y-stratified samples q_j is the proportion of the sample the researcher has decided to obtain and p_i the proportion of X_i that results.

The proportions a, b, c, d are selected to represent the type of association it is critical to detect. To use the χ^2-test at all

$$n \geq 5/\min [p_i q_j, p_i (1 - q_j), (1 - p_i) q_j, (1 - p_i) (1 - q_j)]. \tag{9.1.1}$$

Obviously, rare categories will automatically necessitate a large sample size.

If the sample is X-stratified, the 2 by 2 χ^2-test is essentially a 2-sample binomial test and

$$\delta = 2 [p_i (1 - p_i)]^{1/2} [\arcsin (a/p_i)^{1/2} - \arcsin (c/ (1 - p_i))^{1/2}] \tag{9.1.2}$$

$$\Delta = (e^{2\delta} - 1) / (e^{2\delta} + 1)$$

$$n = v - 1.$$

If the sample is Y stratified, the situation is similar, and

$$\delta = 2 [q_j (1 - q_j)]^{1/2} [\arcsin (a/q_j)^{1/2} - \arcsin (b/ (1 - q_j))^{1/2}] \tag{9.1.3}$$

$$\Delta = (e^{2\delta} - 1) / (e^{2\delta} + 1)$$

$$n = v - 1.$$

If the sample is naturalistic, either of the above calculations is applicable. In this case, the results of the two calculations for Δ rarely differ by more than 0.01.

Whichever n is largest (that from 9.1.1 or that from 9.1.2 or 9.1.3) is the required sample size for that X, Y pair. This process is repeated for each X, Y pair whose association is considered important. The overall recommended sample size is the maximal value of all these sample sizes.

Table 9.1   A 2 by 2 Reduced Table

	Y_j	not Y_j	
X_i	a	b	p_i
Not X_i	c	d	$1 - p_i$
	q_j	$1 - q_j$	

Obviously, sample size must be very large to use a χ^2-test efficiently. The larger the number of categories or the rarer some of the categories, the larger the sample size. For this reason, we recommend that the χ^2-test be used only when there is no other recourse (e.g., the categories cannot be ordered) and, even then, that the number of categories be limited to those essential to the hypothesis. To use the χ^2-test under other circumstances wastes power and entails unnecessary expense.

9.2 An Example of a 3 by 2 Contingency Table Analysis

Suppose, as in Chapter 8, that we wish to determine the association between coffee consumption and the need for non-routine medical care for subjects in their fifties, but this time we wish to distinguish between use of regular and decaffeinated coffee. The variable "coffee consumption" thus corresponds to three categories: none (no), only decaffeinated (decaf), and regular (reg) coffee, which we do not consider to be ordered. The measure of medical care remains a dichotomy (yes or no). The resulting 3 by 2 table can be broken down into three different 2 by 2 comparisons (Table 9.2.1).

The first case corresponds to the hypothesis that coffee use itself is a risk factor, regardless of caffeine content, while the second corresponds to the hypothesis that only coffee with caffeine is associated with an increased need for medical care. The third case, corresponding to the hypothesis that decaffeinated coffee poses risks while drinking regular coffee is no different from abstaining entirely, we do not consider of interest in the present context and dismiss. The necessary sample size is therefore the maximum of that required by the first two cases.

To avoid problems with rare categories (e.g., subjects who drink only decaffeinated coffee), we decide to stratify on coffee consumption, selecting a sample with equal numbers of ordinary coffee drinkers, abstainers, and those who

Table 9.2.1

	Medical Care			Medical Care			Medical Care	
	No	Yes		No	Yes		No	Yes
no			no or decaf			no or reg		
reg or decaf			reg			decaf		

drink only decaffeinated coffee ($p_1, p_2, p_3 \approx 1/3$). As in Chapter 8, we expect that approximately 50% of subjects in their fifties who do not drink coffee at all will seek nonroutine medical care in a given year, and we consider it important to detect a 10% increase in this rate for ordinary coffee drinkers. We expect subjects who drink only decaffeinated coffee to seek care at an intermediate rate. Table 9.2.2, a 3 by 2 table, therefore represents the proportions in the total sample corresponding to the association we consider important to detect. Power calculations are therefore based on the two comparisons of interest (see Table 9.2.3).

As before, we wish to detect an association of this type with 90% power at the 5% level of significance.

In the first case

$$\delta = 2 \, [(.34) \, (.66)]^{1/2} \, (\arcsin(.17/.34)^{1/2} - \arcsin(.28/.66)^{1/2}] = .07,$$

$$\Delta = (e^{2\delta} - 1)/(e^{2\delta} + 1) = .07,$$

$$n = 1744 - 1 = 1743.$$

Table 9.2.2

	Medical Care		
	No	Yes	
No Coffee	0.17	0.17	0.34
Decaffeinated	0.15	0.18	0.33
Regular	0.13	0.20	0.33
	0.45	0.55	

Table 9.2.3

	Medical Care				Medical Care		
	No	Yes			No	Yes	
No Coffee	0.17	0.17	0.34	No or Decaf	0.32	0.35	0.67
Regular or Decaf	0.28	0.38	0.66	Regular	0.13	0.20	0.33
	0.45	0.55			0.45	0.55	

In the second case

$$\delta = 2\,[(.67)\,(.33)]^{1/2}\,(\arcsin(.32/.67)^{1/2} - \arcsin\,(.13/.33)^{1/2} = .08,$$

$$\Delta = (e^{2\delta} - 1)/(e^{2\delta} + 1) = .08,$$

$$n = 1334 - 1 = 1333.$$

The sample size necessary for all comparisons of interest is therefore approximately 1743 or more than twice that required by the binomial test to compare coffee drinkers with abstainers. Expanding the design to include a group of decaffeinated coffee drinkers enables us to answer questions about whether regular coffee poses a greater risk than decaffeinated or whether drinking decaffeinated coffee differs from abstaining from coffee entirely. However, broadening the hypothesis in this way entails studying many more subjects. As always, the researcher must decide whether the value of the additional information justifies the cost of collecting it.

REFERENCES

Lyderson, S., Fagerland, M. W., & Laake, P. (2009). Recommended tests for association in 2 × 2 tables. *Statistics in Medicine, 28,* 1159–1175.

10

Wrap-Up

Obviously, it is not easy to plan successful and cost-effective research projects. Such planning requires a considerable degree of expertise in the field of application, experience, instinct, flexibility, and creativity. Computing a 2 by 2 chi-square test statistic and evaluating its value in a set of data is relatively easy, in fact, trivial with computers. It is considerably more difficult to decide whether the 2 by 2 chi-square test is the best test to use, and if not, what other tests might be appropriate, how many subjects to sample, how to sample them, what measures to use. Furthermore, making a mistake in calculating a test statistic or p-value at the end of a study is easily corrected: One can always redo and correct the calculations. Making a mistake in planning a study as to what data to collect and how many subjects to study is irrevocable. The most painful challenge in statistical consulting is telling researchers who have spent years of time and effort and expended major resources on a research project that the data they collected cannot be used to answer the research question they hoped to answer—that the study has failed.

This book was originally written to allow researchers to include explicit power calculations in the planning of their research projects. However, researchers who know how to do statistical analyses do not necessarily do their own analyses, nor do researchers who know how to do power calculations necessarily take on the onus of all such considerations without statistical consultation. The goals of having a general understanding of the concept of power are much broader. Where earlier discussions of power fail lies in the exclusive emphasis on computation of power, in absence of efforts to make the overall concepts clearer. Those calculations are only a very small, but necessary, part of those concepts. Without appropriate consideration of power, the entire enterprise of applying the scientific method is likely to fail. Power considerations are not the entire enterprise but the linchpin of that enterprise. The following steps are a review of the enterprise.

Step 1: Exploration, Hypothesis Generation

Without thorough exploration leading to the theoretical rationale and empirical justification for a hypothesis, the process is likely to fail. This includes a review of the existing research literature related to the topic of interest, both that related to theory and that related to empirical results. This might include secondary analysis of datasets collected in earlier hypothesis-testing studies, to set the empirical basis for a strong hypothesis. This might include review of clinic records, evaluation of clinical experience, and, yes, the occasional serendipitous finding. This might also mean seeking funding for a hypothesis-generating study when the topic is so close to the cutting-edge of science that little to no research literature or experience is available.

The result of such efforts is not a conclusion but a strong hypothesis to be tested in a future hypothesis-testing study designed for that purpose and the information needed to design such a valid and powerful study. None of this involves statistical tests, p-values, significance levels, or power. If such studies are published, the emphasis is on descriptive statistics and effect sizes.

Should such studies be published? The results of a well-designed, well-executed, well-analyzed study designed to be a hypothesis-generating study, we think, should be published, for it can provide the basis of many future important hypothesis-testing studies. A well-done reanalysis or secondary analysis of the data resulting from a hypothesis-testing study, we think, should be published, provided either it provides the basis of future important hypothesis-testing studies or it raises questions about the validity of previous published reports of the conclusions from the hypothesis-testing study.

Let us take one example: It is our opinion that every randomized clinical trial (RCT) comparing two treatments, T1 versus T2, after the primary research questions are answered according to the a priori plan, should undergo exploratory studies to try to identity moderators and mediators of treatment response (Kraemer, Frank, & Kupfer, 2006). Any moderators or mediators so identified (and there may be many) should be the focus of subsequent RCTs to test those moderators and mediators. Confirmed such moderators would mean that choice of treatment might better be made taking the individual characteristics of patients into account. Confirmed such mediators would provide clues as to how the effectiveness of treatment might be improved or its cost decreased without compromise to effectiveness. In short, the value of RCTs, as they are currently done, would be much enhanced by such exploration and publication of their results.

Currently, the problem is that too much emphasis is placed on p-values and statistical significance. Hypothesis-generating studies, honestly reported as such, are often derided by reviewers of submitted papers, labelled with pejorative terms such as "fishing expeditions," "torturing the data until it confesses," "data dredging," and so forth. The reluctance to publish motivates researchers to present their exploratory results adorned with illegitimate p-values and report the results of post hoc tests as if they were conclusions rather than hypotheses. It is not unusual for reviewers of submitted papers to suggest that the researchers do exactly that, often pointing out which (illegitimate) tests might be used. Ionnidis (2005), in a widely cited article, pointed out in its title that "Most published research findings are false." A great deal of false research findings result when post hoc tests are reported as if they are legitimate hypothesis-testing conclusions.

Similarly, proposals for hypothesis-generating studies, even when absolutely necessary to open up a new field, are not positively viewed by proposal reviewers, who want assurance that answers, not questions, will result from the proposed study. Yet the cost of such reluctance is that hypothesis-testing studies are often premature (weak rationale and justification) and poorly designed (inadequate power). To get such studies funded, researchers feel obliged to present their hypothesis-generating proposals as if they are hypothesis testing, frequently with multiple testing the sole cue that there are only weak theoretical grounds and no empirical justification for the hypotheses presented. Since the information necessary to design powerful studies to test those "hypotheses" is unavailable, most of the testing is likely to fail. With multiple testing, there are likely to be many false positives, which can mislead further research. The time and resources invested in such studies is wasted. Again, reviewers of proposals often suggest poorly conceived hypothesis testing, asking researchers, for example, to "control" for all sorts of baseline factors in an RCT without any rationale or justification to hypothesize any association between those factors and treatment response, much less the nature of such an association. Inclusion of irrelevant factors can often lead to misleading results.

To make matters even worse, if a hypothesis-testing study is proposed citing a well-done hypothesis-generating study as empirical justification for the hypothesis, reviewers are often reluctant to fund the study, taking that empirical justification as evidence that the conclusion has already been reached. It must be stressed that exploration leads to many false positives, and that, in absence of hypothesis-testing studies that provide confirmation for that hypothesis, such a result cannot be taken as fact.

How much better it would be if the necessity for excellent hypothesis-generating studies were simply acknowledged, and the criteria for judging the quality of such proposed studies or the research reports resulting from such studies were clearly distinguished from the criteria for judging the quality of hypothesis-testing studies. At the same time, any proposal for a hypothesis-testing study that is not based on sound hypothesis-generating studies should be rejected as premature or ill advised. Any paper that reports post hoc analyses as if they were hypothesis testing should be regarded as scientific malpractice.

Step 2: Design of a Hypothesis-Testing Study

Once there is the appropriate basis for proposing a hypothesis-testing study, the trick then is to design a study to test that hypothesis. What population is of interest and how might one access a representative sample from that population? Should the sample be naturalistic, or should it be stratified? Can a cross-sectional design validly test the hypothesis, or is a longitudinal design necessary? If a longitudinal design is necessary, how long should follow-up be and how frequently should participants be seen during that follow-up? What baseline data are necessary both to describe the population and to provide necessary information to understand the results (e.g., possibly moderators of treatment response in an RCT)? How is it best to measure the outcome? What other information during follow-up is necessary to understand the results (e.g., possible mediators of treatment response in an RCT)? Once these decisions are in place, what analytic procedure would test the hypothesis to produce valid results and yield the greatest power to detect effect sizes of practical and clinical significance? Only then, once all these decisions are made, how many subjects are necessary for adequate power?

It should be emphasized that there are likely to be multiple research designs and associated tests that would provide valid results. Power considerations then are very useful to choose among these valid tests the one most feasible and cost effective.

For example, there is often the option of using a continuous outcome (e.g., degree of symptom reduction) or a dichotomization (e.g., at least a 50% reduction: yes/no). Almost without exception there is a major loss of power in using the dichotomization. In some cases, use of dichotomized outcome would require increasing the sample size by a factor of 2 or 3. Using the continuous outcome is almost always preferable. But, one may use the continuous outcome only at the endpoint, or one might consider a pre-post change, or one might consider measuring the outcome at the pretreatment, the post-treatment, and several intermediate time points. If the measure of outcome has poor reliability, a pre-post change would mean reduction of power. If the measure has good reliability, it would mean greater power. Having several intermediate points would increase power, and having enough, properly spaced, would almost always increase power above that with the endpoint or pre-post change design. How many such intermediate points are needed depends on the reliability of the outcome measure.

But of course, some outcome measures are natural dichotomies, for example, status at the end of treatment: alive/dead. However, two study participants may both be dead five years after start of treatment, but one may have died after one week and the other just at five years. Use of the dichotomy does not distinguish these two, but certainly a patient and his clinicians would prefer that she or he live five years rather than one week! If, instead of using the dichotomy (alive/dead at five years), one compared instead the distribution of time to death, a continuous measure, one would gain power, thereby necessitating a smaller sample size as well as gaining greater sensitivity to crucially important individual differences between participants.

To test the efficacy/effectiveness of a treatment in a general population, a naturalistic sample is best. If one chooses to stratify, to match, or to use certain baseline variables as covariates, this might mean losing the ability to test the overall effectiveness in favor of testing in certain subpopulations, or it might mean loss of power, thus necessitating an increased sample size.

In any hypothesis-testing study, the more reliable the measures used, the greater the power, and thus the smaller the sample size necessary for adequate power. If, instead of using a single measure of the outcome one used the average of multiple independent measures of that outcome, one would increase the reliability of the measure of outcome and thus increase the power and reduce the necessary sample size.

How do we know or learn such facts? The answers lie in power computations in designing research studies. Such a list of insights can go on and on, but the crucial factor is that each entry into this list is simply based on comparing the power curves that result from different proposals for design and analysis. Those that carefully consider power issues in designing their studies are often subliminally training themselves to design better studies now and in the future.

Step 3: A Pilot Study?

As we noted much earlier, the term *pilot study* is often used as a synonym for a poorly designed, underpowered, hypothesis-testing study. This is unfortunate, first, because such studies would do less damage were they honestly labelled as "badly done studies," and second, because the original use of the term pilot study, referring to feasibility studies for subsequent hypothesis-testing studies, pertains to a very important step in the research progress that otherwise may be overlooked.

When a hypothesis-testing study is designed, there are often strategies proposed that may or may not be feasible, either in general or in the particular milieu in which the study is to be done. To check these out in a small preliminary study, keeping open the option of modifying strategies that prove unfeasible prevents finding the bad news out after the study is started. If such problems are identified after the hypothesis-testing study is begun, this too often leads to failed studies and loss of time, effort, and resources, which often results in misleading results reported in the literature.

Not every hypothesis-testing study requires a pilot study. If the researchers proposing the study have long worked in a particular research area, they may well fully know what is or is not feasible and can cite their own previous work in that area to demonstrate to proposal reviewers that what they propose is feasible. However, if there are feasibility questions, it is far better to expend a small amount of time and resources to prevent expending major time and resources, only to fail.

A common error is to propose a pilot study in order to estimate the true effect size to be used as the critical effect size in the subsequent power computation for the hypothesis-testing study. This is a serious error (Kraemer, Mintz, Noda, Tinklenberg, & Yesavage, 2006). First of all, the critical effect size is the *threshold* of clinical or practical significance. The rationale and justification for a hypothesis-testing study should strongly suggest that the true effect size is larger, sometimes much larger, than the critical effect size. The estimated effect size from a pilot study is based on a very small sample size and is therefore a very inaccurate estimate of the true effect size, very likely to be grossly overestimated or underestimated. If it is overestimated, the sample size one would project as necessary may be far beyond what is possible; if it is underestimated, the sample size one would project as necessary may be far below what is needed. If there is overestimation, the study may well be aborted, and if there is underestimation, the study may be funded and undertaken but is likely to be underpowered and to fail. There is no positive outcome from using an inaccurately estimated true effect size as the critical effect size in determining sample size. The critical effect size is crucial.

Step 4: Doing the Proposed Hypothesis-Testing Study With Fidelity

Once a hypothesis-testing study is underway, the a priori plan should be followed exactly: no tweaking of inclusion/exclusion criteria, no substitution or addition of measures, no changes in protocols, and so forth. Yes, this is easier said than done, but the less deviation, the more likely a clear and convincing answer to the original research question, and the less likely a failed study.

Researchers should be encouraged to report the results of studies, both exploratory and confirmatory, in terms of effect sizes and their confidence intervals. The results of a study should be described in sufficient statistical detail that they can be used in planning any further studies of the same hypothesis or of related issues in the same field. Results should never be reported only in terms of "NS" or one, two, or three asterisks. These are uninformative symbols, giving no specific information as to what is going on.

Step 5: Independent Confirmation/Replication (Meta-Analysis)

Finally it must be understood that a positive conclusion from a single hypothesis-testing study does not establish scientific fact; it only provides support to the hypothesis. Until there is independent replication or validation, the conclusion is not definitive. We can argue as to how many positive studies are needed to establish scientific fact, but the most direct route to an answer is via meta-analysis. Once, considering all studies done on a particular issue, there is reasonable homogeneity among the effect sizes, and the confidence interval for the pooled effect size lies completely above the critical value, that is definitive: The hypothesis may be regarded as scientific fact. If there is reasonable homogeneity among the effect sizes, and the confidence interval for the pooled effect size lies completely below the limits of the critical value, that too is definitive: The hypothesis may not be completely false (null hypothesis true) but, even if true, is not of any clinical or practical significance. If neither of these situations pertains, further studies may be needed, and the information in the studies included in the meta-analysis provides guidance as to how best to design such studies. If there is not reasonable homogeneity, the sources of heterogeneity may have to be identified for further studies to be more successful.

Since meta-analysis is determined by the number of studies available—power considerations do not apply. However, there is a problem related to inclusion of underpowered individual studies in meta-analysis, related to the "file drawer problem" (Rosenthal, 1979). It has long been suspected that "statistically significant" results are more likely to be published than are "non-statistically significant" results. Once again, this results from that overemphasis on p-values. To take an extreme view, if the hypothesis were false (the null hypothesis true), of all studies done at the 5% significance level, the 5% that resulted in false positive results would be published, and the remaining 95% would end in the "file drawer" inaccessible to the meta-analyst. Estimating the true effect size from the published 5% studies would generally overestimate the true effect size and mislead conclusions.

Actually the situation is not quite as bad as that. Generally, large research studies (adequately powered studies) are likely to be published whatever their findings. But the risk of a biased conclusion still remains. One way to handle this is to include in the criteria for inclusion in the meta-analysis, a criterion for adequate power. That is, published studies that are underpowered by the meta-analysts' a priori criterion would be excluded from the meta-analysis. This does not eliminate the bias because of the file drawer problem but substantially reduces it (Kraemer, Gardner, Brooks, & Yesavage, 1998). Excluding such studies might also have the effect of discouraging researchers from doing such studies.

Currently, many researchers justify doing badly designed, underpowered studies by the claim that, while their study might not be in itself definitive, it might contribute to a definitive finding when combined with other studies (i.e., via meta-analysis). The evidence, however, shows that such studies detract from reaching a definitive finding and should be discouraged.

A few final words: It is not a minor problem that those who are able to do power calculations readily are generally those who least know the fields of application, and those who best know the fields of application are least able to do power calculations. When seeking statistical consultation, such issues of particular and specific relevance in the researchers' own fields of research may never be brought to the attention of the consulting statistician. A consulting statistician not versed in psychiatric diagnosis, for example, may not know that there are several extant valid and reliable scales measuring severity of clinical depression. The possibility of using such a scale rather than a depressed/nondepressed dichotomy in a clinical drug trial then may simply not arise for discussion. The researcher is then informed that 500 patients are needed and never realize that 50 might otherwise have sufficed. In short, the most cost-effective decisions are not necessarily the ones made, even with expert advice. They are the ones made by effective communication among multiple researchers with different knowledge and skill sets.

Consequently, we feel that the most beneficial effect of a clearer understanding of power considerations is to alert researchers to the kinds and range of issues involved in planning powerful research studies and to clarify communication among researchers themselves and with their statistical consultants.

REFERENCES

Ioannidis, J. P. A. (2005). Why most published research findings are false. *PLoS Medicine*, *2*(8), 696–791.

Kraemer, H. C., Frank, E., & Kupfer, D. J. (2006). Moderators of treatment outcomes: Clinical, research, and policy importance. *Journal of the American Medical Association*, *296*(10), 1–4.

Kraemer, H. C., Gardner, C., Brooks, J. O., & Yesavage, J. A. (1998). The advantages of excluding under-powered studies in meta-analysis: Inclusionist versus exclusionist viewpoints. *Psychological Methods*, *3*, 23–31.

Kraemer, H. C., Mintz, J., Noda, A., Tinklenberg, J., & Yesavage, J. A. (2006). Caution regarding the use of pilot studies to guide power calculations for study proposals. *Archives of General Psychiatry*, *63*(5), 484–489.

Rosenthal, R. (1979). The "file drawer problem" and tolerance for null results. *Psychological Bulletin, 86*, 638–641.

Summary Table

Test	Specification	H_0	ν	Δ	Section
Single-Sample Normal Test	$X_i \sim N(\mu, \sigma^2)$ $i = 1, 2, \ldots, n$ σ^2 known	$\mu = \mu_0$	$n + 1$	$\Delta = (e^{2\delta} - 1)/(e^{2\delta} + 1)$ $\delta = (\mu - \mu_0)/\sigma$	4.1
Single-Sample t Matched Pair t	$X_i \sim N(\mu, \sigma^2)$	$\mu = \mu_0$	$n - 1$	$\Delta = \delta/(\delta^2 + 1)^{1/2}$	4.2
Two-Sample t	$i = 1, 2, \ldots, n$ $X_i \sim N(\mu_x, \sigma^2)$ $i = 1, 2, \ldots, np$ $Y_i \sim N(\mu_y, \sigma^2)$ $i = 1, 2, \ldots, nq$ $p + q = 1$	$\mu_x = \mu_y$	$n - 2$	$\delta = (\mu - \mu_0)/\sigma$ $\Delta = \delta/(\delta^2 + 1/pq)^{1/2}$ $\delta = (\mu_x - \mu_y)/\sigma$	4.3
Intraclass ρ	$(x_i y_i)$ Bivariate Normal corr $(X_i, Y_i) = \rho$ $i = 1, 2, \ldots, n$ $\sigma_x^2 = \sigma_y^2$	$\rho = \rho_0$	$n - 1$	$\Delta = (\rho - \rho_0)/(1 - \rho\rho_0)$	5.1
Product-Moment ρ	$(x_i y_i)$ Bivariate Normal corr $(X_i, Y_i) = \rho$ $i = 1, 2, \ldots, n$	$\rho = \rho_0$	$n - 2$	$\Delta = (\rho - \rho_0)/(1 - \rho\rho_0)$	5.2

(Continued)

113

Test	Specification	H_0	ν	Δ	Section
Spearman ρ	(x_i, y_i) Bivariate Normal corr $(X_i, Y_i) = \rho$ $i = 1,2,\ldots,n$	$\rho = \rho_0$	$(n-3)/1.060$	$\Delta = \frac{6}{\pi}[\arcsin(\rho/2) - \arcsin(\rho_0/2)]$	5.3
Kendall ρ	(x_i, y_i) Bivariate Normal corr $(X_i, Y_i) = \rho$ $i = 1,2,\ldots,n$	$\rho = \rho_0$	$(n-4)/.437$	$\Delta = \frac{2}{\pi}[\arcsin(\rho) - \arcsin(\rho_0)]$	5.3
Linear Regression	$Y_i \sim \alpha + \beta X_i + \varepsilon_i$ $i = 1,2,\ldots,n$ $\varepsilon_i \sim N(0,\sigma_\varepsilon^2)$ X_i regarded as fixed with some variance s_x^2	$\beta = \beta_0$	$n-2$	$\Delta = \delta/(\delta^2+1/s_x^2)^{1/2}$ $\delta = (\beta - \beta_0)/\sigma_\varepsilon$	6.1
Variance Ratio Test Independent Samples	$X_i \sim N(\mu_x, \sigma_x^2)$ $1 = 1,2,\ldots,np$ $Y_i \sim N(\mu_y, \sigma_y^2)$ $1 = 1,2,\ldots,np$ $P + 1=1$	$\sigma_x^2 = \sigma_y^2$	$\dfrac{(2n^2\, pq-3n+4)}{(n-2)}$	$\Delta = (\sigma_x^2 - \sigma_y^2)/(\sigma_x^2 + \sigma_y^2)$	7.1

Test	Specification	H_0	ν	Δ	Section
Variance Ratio Test Matched Samples	(x_i, y_i) Bivariate Normal corr $(X_i, Y_i) = \rho$ $i = 1,2,\ldots,n$	$\sigma_x^2 = \sigma_y^2$	$n - 2$	$\Delta = (\sigma_x^2 - \sigma_y^2)/[(\sigma_x^2 + \sigma_y^2)^2 - 4\rho^2\sigma_x^2\sigma_y^2]^{1/2}$	7.2
Sign, Median, or Single Sample Binomial	$X_i \sim B(n, \pi)$ $i = 1,2,\ldots,np$	$\pi = \pi_0$	$n + 1$	$\Delta = (e^{2\delta} - 1)/(e^{2\delta} + 1)$ $\delta = 2[\arcsin \pi^{1/2} - \arcsin (\pi_0^{1/2})]$	8.1
Two-Sample Binomial Test ($2 \times 2\ \chi^2$ Stratified)	$X_i \sim B(\pi_x)$ $i=1,2,\ldots,np$ $Y_i \sim B(\pi_y)$ $i = 1,2,\ldots,np$ $p + q = 1$	$\pi_x = \pi_y$	$n + 1$	$\Delta = (e^{2\delta} - 1)/(e^{2\delta} + 1)$ $\delta = 2(pq)^{1/2}[\arcsin\pi_x^{1/2} - \arcsin \pi_y^{1/2}]$	8.2

Master Table

Δ	POWER										
	99	95	90	80	70	60	50	40	30	20	10
0.01	157695	108215	85634	61823	47055	36031	27055	19363	12555	6453	1321
0.02	39417	27050	21405	15454	11763	9007	6764	4841	3139	1614	331
0.03	17514	12019	9511	6867	5227	4003	3006	2152	1396	718	148
0.04	9848	6758	5348	3861	2939	2251	1691	1210	785	404	84
0.05	6299	4323	3421	2470	1881	1440	1082	775	503	259	54
0.06	4372	3000	2375	1715	1305	1000	751	538	349	180	38
0.07	3209	2203	1744	1259	959	734	552	395	257	133	29
0.08	2455	1685	1334	963	734	562	422	303	197	102	23
0.09	1938	1330	1053	761	579	444	334	239	156	81	18
0.10	1568	1076	852	616	469	359	270	194	126	66	15
0.11	1294	889	704	508	387	297	223	160	104	54	13
0.12	1086	746	590	427	325	249	188	135	88	46	11
0.13	924	635	503	363	277	212	160	115	75	39	10
0.14	796	546	433	313	238	183	138	99	65	34	.

(Continued)

117

5% Level, One-Tailed Test (Continued)

						POWER					
Δ	99	95	90	80	70	60	50	40	30	20	10
0.15	692	475	376	272	207	159	120	86	56	30	.
0.16	607	417	330	239	182	140	105	76	50	27	.
0.17	537	369	292	211	161	124	93	67	44	24	.
0.18	478	328	260	188	144	110	83	60	39	21	.
0.19	428	294	233	169	129	99	75	54	35	19	.
0.20	385	265	210	152	116	89	67	49	32	17	.
0.22	317	218	173	125	96	74	56	40	27	15	.
0.24	265	182	144	105	80	62	47	34	23	12	.
0.26	224	154	122	89	68	52	40	29	19	11	.
0.28	192	132	105	76	58	45	34	25	17	10	.
0.30	166	114	91	66	51	39	30	22	15	.	.
0.32	145	100	79	58	44	34	26	19	13	.	.
0.34	127	88	70	51	39	30	23	17	12	.	.
0.36	113	78	62	45	35	27	20	15	10	.	.

POWER

Δ	99	95	90	80	70	60	50	40	30	20	10
0.38	100	69	55	40	31	24	18	14	.	.	.
0.40	89	62	49	36	28	21	16	12	.	.	.
0.45	69	48	38	28	21	17	13	10	.	.	.
0.50	54	37	30	22	17	13	10	.	.	.	.
0.55	43	30	24	17	14	11	.	.	.	.	.
0.60	34	24	19	14	11	.	.	.	.	.	.
0.65	28	19	16	12	.	.	.	.	.	.	.
0.70	23	16	13	10	.	.	.	.	.	.	.
0.75	18	13	10	.	.	.	.	.	.	.	.
0.80	15	10	.	.	.	.	.	.	.	.	.
0.85	12	.	.	.	.	.	.	.	.	.	.
0.90	.	.	.	.	.	.	.	.	.	.	.

1% Level, One-Tailed Test

					POWER						
Δ	99	95	90	80	70	60	50	40	30	20	10
0.01	216463	157695	130162	100355	81264	66545	54117	42972	32469	22044	10917
0.02	54106	39417	32535	25085	20313	16634	13528	10742	8117	5511	2730
0.03	24040	17514	14456	11146	9026	7391	6011	4773	3607	2449	1214
0.04	13517	9848	8128	6267	5075	4156	3380	2684	2029	1378	683
0.05	8646	6299	5200	4009	3247	2659	2163	1718	1298	882	437
0.06	6000	4372	3609	2783	2254	1846	1501	1192	901	612	304
0.07	4405	3209	2649	2043	1655	1355	1102	876	662	450	224
0.08	3369	2455	2027	1563	1266	1037	843	670	507	344	171
0.09	2660	1938	1600	1234	999	819	666	529	400	272	136
0.10	2152	1568	1295	998	809	663	539	428	324	220	110
0.11	1776	1294	1069	824	668	547	445	354	268	182	91
0.12	1490	1086	897	692	560	459	374	297	225	153	77
0.13	1268	924	763	589	477	391	318	253	191	130	65
0.14	1092	796	657	507	411	337	274	218	165	112	56

POWER

Δ	10	20	30	40	50	60	70	80	90	95	99
0.15	49	98	144	190	238	293	357	441	571	692	949
0.16	43	86	126	166	209	257	314	387	501	607	833
0.17	39	76	112	147	185	277	277	342	443	537	736
0.18	34	68	100	131	165	202	247	305	395	478	655
0.19	31	61	89	118	148	181	221	273	353	428	587
0.20	29	55	81	106	133	163	199	246	318	385	528
0.22	24	46	66	87	110	135	164	202	262	317	434
0.24	21	38	56	73	92	113	137	169	219	265	363
0.26	18	33	47	62	78	95	116	143	185	224	307
0.28	16	29	41	53	67	82	100	123	159	192	263
0.30	14	25	35	46	58	71	86	106	137	166	227
0.32	12	22	31	41	51	62	75	93	120	145	198
0.34	11	20	28	36	45	55	66	82	105	127	174
0.36	10	18	25	32	40	48	59	72	93	113	154
0.38	.	16	22	29	35	43	52	64	83	100	137

(Continued)

121

Δ	99	95	90	80	70	60	50	40	30	20	10
						POWER					
0.40	122	89	74	57	47	39	32	26	20	15	.
0.45	94	69	57	44	36	30	25	20	16	12	.
0.50	73	54	45	35	29	24	20	16	13	.	.
0.55	58	43	36	28	23	19	16	13	11	.	.
0.60	47	34	29	23	19	16	13	11	.	.	.
0.65	38	28	23	18	15	13	11	.	.	.	.
0.70	30	23	19	15	12	11	.	.	.	.	.
0.75	25	18	15	12	10	.	.	.	.	.	.
0.80	20	15	12	10	.	.	.	.	.	.	.
0.85	16	12	10	.	.	.	.	.	.	.	.
0.90	12	.	.	.							

Δ	POWER										
	99	95	90	80	70	60	50	40	30	20	10
0.01	183714	129940	105069	78485	61718	48986	38414	29125	20609	12508	4604
0.02	45920	32480	26263	19618	15428	12245	9603	7281	5152	3127	1152
0.03	20403	14431	11669	8717	6855	5441	4267	3236	2290	1390	513
0.04	11472	8115	6562	4902	3855	3060	2400	1820	1288	782	289
0.05	7338	5191	4197	3136	2466	1958	1536	1165	824	501	185
0.06	5093	3602	2913	2177	1712	1359	1066	809	573	348	129
0.07	3739	2645	2139	1598	1257	998	783	594	421	256	95
0.08	2860	2023	1636	1223	962	764	599	455	322	196	73
0.09	2257	1597	1292	965	759	603	473	359	255	155	58
0.10	1826	1292	1045	781	615	488	383	291	206	126	47
0.11	1508	1067	863	645	507	403	316	240	170	104	39
0.12	1265	895	724	541	426	338	266	202	143	88	33
0.13	1076	762	616	461	363	288	226	172	122	75	29
0.14	927	656	531	397	312	248	195	148	105	64	25

(Continued)

5% Level, Two-Tailed Test (Continued)

Δ	99	95	90	80	70	60	50	40	30	20	10
						POWER					
0.15	806	570	461	345	272	216	170	129	92	56	22
0.16	707	500	405	303	238	190	149	113	81	50	20
0.17	625	442	358	268	211	168	132	100	71	44	18
0.18	556	394	319	238	188	149	117	89	64	39	16
0.19	498	353	286	214	168	134	105	80	57	35	15
0.20	449	318	257	192	152	121	95	72	52	32	13
0.22	369	261	212	158	125	99	78	60	43	27	11
0.24	308	218	177	133	105	83	66	50	36	23	10
0.26	261	185	150	112	89	71	56	43	31	20	.
0.28	223	159	128	96	76	61	48	37	27	17	.
0.30	193	137	111	83	66	53	42	32	23	15	.
0.32	169	120	97	73	58	46	36	28	21	13	.
0.34	148	105	85	64	51	41	32	25	18	12	.

POWER

Δ	99	95	90	80	70	60	50	40	30	20	10
0.36	131	93	75	57	45	36	29	22	16	11	.
0.38	116	83	67	51	40	32	26	20	15	10	.
0.40	104	74	60	45	36	29	23	18	13	.	.
0.45	80	57	46	35	28	22	18	14	11	.	.
0.50	62	45	36	27	22	18	14	11	.	.	.
0.55	50	35	29	22	18	14	12	.	.	.	.
0.60	40	29	23	18	14	12	10	.	.	.	.
0.65	32	23	19	15	12	10	.	.	.	.	.
0.70	26	19	15	12	10	.	.	.	.	.	.
0.75	21	15	13	10	.	.	.	.	.	.	.
0.80	17	12	10	.	.	.	.	.	.	.	.
0.85	13	10	.	.	.	.	.	.	.	.	.
0.90	10	.	.	.	.	.	.	.	.	.	.

1% Level, Two-Tailed Test

Δ						POWER					
	99	95	90	80	70	60	50	40	30	20	10
0.01	240299	178131	148785	116783	96109	80039	66346	55937	42082	30074	16752
0.02	60064	44525	37190	29191	24024	20007	16584	13483	10520	7518	4188
0.03	26687	19783	16524	12970	10674	8890	7369	5991	4675	3341	1862
0.04	15005	11123	9291	7293	6002	4999	4144	3369	2629	1879	1047
0.05	9598	7115	5943	4665	3840	3198	2651	2155	1682	1202	670
0.06	6661	4938	4125	3238	2665	2220	1840	1496	1168	835	466
0.07	4890	3625	3028	2377	1957	1630	1351	1099	858	613	342
0.08	3740	2773	2316	1819	1497	1247	1034	841	656	469	262
0.09	2952	2189	1829	1436	1182	984	816	664	518	371	207
0.10	2389	1771	1480	1162	956	797	661	537	420	300	168
0.11	1972	1462	1221	959	789	658	545	444	346	248	139
0.12	1654	1227	1025	805	663	552	458	372	291	208	117
0.13	1407	1044	872	685	564	470	390	317	248	177	100
0.14	1212	898	751	590	485	405	336	273	213	153	86

					POWER						
Δ	99	95	90	80	70	60	50	40	30	20	10
0.15	1054	781	653	513	422	352	292	238	186	133	75
0.16	924	685	573	450	371	309	256	209	163	117	66
0.17	817	606	506	398	328	273	227	185	144	104	58
0.18	727	539	451	354	292	243	202	164	129	92	52
0.19	651	483	404	317	261	218	181	147	115	83	47
0.20	586	435	364	286	235	196	163	133	104	75	42
0.22	482	358	299	235	194	162	134	109	86	62	35
0.24	403	299	250	196	162	135	112	92	72	52	30
0.26	341	253	212	166	137	115	95	78	61	44	26
0.28	292	217	181	143	118	98	82	67	52	38	23
0.30	252	187	157	123	102	85	71	58	45	33	20
0.32	220	163	137	108	89	74	62	51	40	30	18
0.34	193	144	120	95	78	65	54	45	35	26	15

(Continued)

POWER

Δ	99	95	90	80	70	60	50	40	30	20	10
0.36	171	127	106	84	69	58	48	39	31	24	15
0.38	152	113	94	74	62	52	43	35	29	21	13
0.40	135	101	84	67	55	46	38	32	26	19	12
0.45	104	77	65	51	42	36	30	25	20	15	10
0.50	81	61	51	40	33	28	24	20	16	12	.
0.55	64	48	40	32	27	23	19	16	13	10	.
0.60	52	39	32	26	22	19	16	15	11	.	.
0.65	41	31	27	21	18	15	13	11	.	.	.
0.70	33	25	22	17	15	13	11	.	.	.	.
0.75	27	21	17	14	12	10	.	.	.	.	.
0.80	22	17	14	11	.	.	.	.	.	.	.
0.85	17	13	11	.	.	.	.	.	.	.	.
0.90	13	10	.	.	.	.	.	.	.	.	.

References

Acion, L., Peterson, J. J., Temple, S., & Arndt, S. (2006). Probabilistic index: An intuitive non-parametric approach to measuring the size of treatment effects. *Statistics in Medicine, 25*(4), 591–602.

Baron, R. M., & Kenny, D. A. (1986). The moderator-mediator variable distinction in social psychological research: Conceptual, strategic, and statistical considerations. *Journal of Personality and Social Psychology, 51*, 1173–1182.

Bartko, J. J. (1976). On various intraclass correlation reliability coefficients. *Psychological Bulletin, 83*, 762–765.

Boomsma, A. (1977). Comparing approximations of confidence intervals for the product-moment correlation coefficient. *Statistica Neerlandica, 31*, 179–185.

Brown, B. W., Jr. (1980). The crossover experiment for clinical trials. *Biometrics, 36*, 69–79.

Brown, W. (1910). Some experimental results in the correlation of mental abilities. *British Journal of Psychology, 3*, 296–322.

Campbell, D. T., & Kenny, D. A. (1999). *A primer on regression artifacts.* New York: Guilford Press.

Chan, A. W., Hrobjartsson, A., Haahr, M. T., Gotzsche, P. C., & Altman, D. G. (2004). Empirical evidence for selective reporting of outcome in randomized trials. *Journal of the American Medical Association, 291*(20), 2457–2465.

Chaubey, Y. P., & Mudholkar, G. S. (1978). A new approximation for Fisher's Z. *Australian Journal of Statistics, 20*, 250–256.

Cohen, J. (1983). The cost of dichotomization. *Applied Psychological Measurement, 7*(3), 249–253.

Cohen, J. (1988). *Statistical power analysis for the behavioral sciences.* Hillsdale, NJ: Lawrence Erlbaum.

Cooper, H., & Hedges, L. V. (1994). *The handbook of research synthesis.* New York: Russell Sage.

Cumming, G. (2012). *Understanding the new statistics: Effect sizes, confidence intervals, and meta-analysis.* New York: Routledge.

DeCoster, J., & Iselin, A.-M. R. (2009). A conceptual and empirical examination of justifications for dichotomization. *Psychological Methods, 14*(4), 349–366.

Ellis, P. D. (2010). *The essential guide to effect sizes*. New York: Cambridge University Press.

Fisher, R. A. (1921). On the "probable error" of a coefficient of correlation deduced from a small sample. *Metron, 1*, 1–32.

Fisher, R. A , & Yates, F. (1957). *Statistical tables for biological, agricultural and medical research*. London: Oliver and Boyd.

Freedman, B. (1987). Equipoise and the ethics of clinical research. *The New England Journal of Medicine, 317*, 141–145.

Goldstein, A. (1964). *Biostatistics: An introductory text*. New York: McMillan.

Grissom, R. J., & Kim, J. J. (2012). *Effect sizes for research: Univariate and multivariate applicatioins*. New York: Routledge.

Haggard, E. A. (1958). *Intraclass correlation and the analysis of variance*. New York: Dryden Press.

Ioannidis, J. P. A. (2005). Why most published research findings are false. *PLoS Medicine, 2*(8), 696–791.

Jones, D. R. (1995). Meta-analysis: Weighing the evidence. *Statistics in Medicine, 14*, 137–149.

Kowalski, C. J. (1972). On the effects on non-normality on the distribution of the sample correlation coefficient. *The Journal of the Royal Statistical Society, 21*, 1–12.

Kraemer, H. C. (1975). On estimation and hypothesis testing problems for correlation coefficients. *Psychometrika, 40*(4), 473–485.

Kraemer, H. C. (1980). Robustness of the distribution theory of the product-moment correlation coefficient. *Journal of Educational Statistics, 5*(2), 115–128.

Kraemer, H. C., & Blasey, C. (2004). Centring in regression analysis: A strategy to prevent errors in statistical inference. *International Journal of Methods in Psychiatric Research, 13*(3), 141–151.

Kraemer, H. C., Frank, E., & Kupfer, D. J. (2006). Moderators of treatment outcomes: Clinical, research, and policy importance. *Journal of the American Medical Association, 296*(10), 1–4.

Kraemer, H. C., Gardner, C., Brooks, J. O., & Yesavage, J. A. (1998). The advantages of excluding under-powered studies in meta-analysis: Inclusionist versus exclusionist viewpoints. *Psychological Methods, 3*, 23–31.

Kraemer, H. C., Kazdin, A. E., Offord, D. R., Kessler, R. C., Jensen, P. S., & Kupfer, D. J. (1997). Coming to terms with the terms of risk. *Archives of General Psychiatry, 54*, 337–343.

Kraemer, H. C., & Kupfer, D. J. (2006). Size of treatment effects and their importance to clinical research and practice. *Biological Psychiatry, 59*(11), 990–996.

Kraemer, H. C., Mintz, J., Noda, A., Tinklenberg, J., & Yesavage, J. A. (2006). Caution regarding the use of pilot studies to guide power calculations for study proposals. *Archives of General Psychiatry, 63*(5), 484–489.

Kraemer, H. C., & Paik, M. A. (1979). A central t approximation to the noncentral t-distribution. *Technometrics, 21*(3), 357–360.

Kraemer, H. C., & Thiemann, S. A. (1989). A strategy to use "soft" data effectively in randomized clinical trials. *Journal of Consulting and Clinical Psychology, 57*, 148–154.

Last, J. M. (1995). *A dictionary of epidemiology*. New York: Oxford University Press.

Lyderson, S., Fagerland, M. W., & Laake, P. (2009). Recommended tests for association in 2X2 tables. *Statistics in Medicine, 28,* 1159–1175.

MacCallum, R. C., Zhang, S., Preacher, K. J., & Rucker, D. D. (2002). On the practice of dichotomization of quantitative variables. *Psychological Methods, 7*(1), 19–40.

McGough, J. J., & Faraone, S. V. (2009). Estimating the size of treatment effects: Moving beyond *p* values. *Psychiatry (Edgmont), 6*(10), 21–29.

Morgan, W. A. (1939). A test for the significance of the difference between the two variances in a sample from a normal bivariate population. *Biometrika, 31,* 13–19.

Pearson, E. S., & Hartley, H. O. (1962). *Biometrika tables for statisticians* (Vol. 1). Cambridge: Cambridge University Press.

Peto, R. (1981). The horse-racing effect. *Lancet, 318*(8244), 467–468.

Pitman, E. J. G. (1939). A note on normal correlation. *Biometrika, 31,* 9–12.

Rosenthal, R. (1979). The "file drawer problem" and tolerance for null results. *Psychological Bulletin, 86,* 638–641.

Royston, P., Altman, D. G., & Sauerbrei, W. (2006). Dichotomizing continuous predictors in multiple regression: A bad idea. *Statistics in Medicine, 25,* 127–141.

Spearman, C. (1910). Correlation calculated from faulty data. *British Journal of Psychology, 3,* 271–295.

Index

⑤SAGE researchmethods

The essential online tool for researchers from the world's leading methods publisher

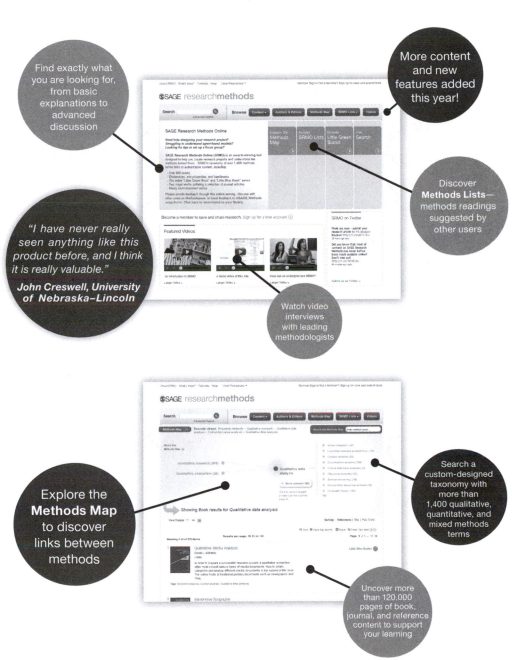

Find exactly what you are looking for, from basic explanations to advanced discussion

More content and new features added this year!

"I have never really seen anything like this product before, and I think it is really valuable."

John Creswell, University of Nebraska–Lincoln

Discover **Methods Lists**— methods readings suggested by other users

Watch video interviews with leading methodologists

Explore the **Methods Map** to discover links between methods

Search a custom-designed taxonomy with more than 1,400 qualitative, quantitative, and mixed methods terms

Uncover more than 120,000 pages of book, journal, and reference content to support your learning

Find out more at
www.sageresearchmethods.com